GRACE
THUS
FAR

◆

David H. C. Read

WILLIAM B. EERDMANS PUBLISHING COMPANY
GRAND RAPIDS, MICHIGAN

Copyright © 1986 by Wm. B. Eerdmans Publishing Co.
255 Jefferson Ave. S.E., Grand Rapids, Mich. 49503
All rights reserved
Printed in the United States of America

Library of Congress Cataloging-in-Publication Data

Read, David Haxton Carswell.
Grace thus far.

1. Read, David Haxton Carswell.
2. Presbyterian Church (U.S.A.) — Clergy — Biography.
3. Presbyterian Church — United States — Clergy — Biography.
I. Title.
BX9225.R36A3   1986   285'.137'0924 [B]   86-16784

ISBN 0-8028-0245-1

Contents

Introduction

It will be obvious to any reader, from the very first page, that this book is a sequel. In *This Grace Given* (published in 1984) I rambled over the first thirty-five years of my life, from my ancestry ("The God in Our Genes") to my liberation from a P.O.W. camp in 1945 ("An Ultimate Grace").

That moment was climactic in this man's experience of the grace of God. But there was more to come—over the next forty years, in fact. So I felt it necessary to ramble on to the present day and offer these reflections with the title *Grace Thus Far*, encouraged by readers who wanted to know something about those postwar years.

This book covers my ministry in Scotland, first as preacher in a suburban church and then as chaplain to Edinburgh University. It deals inevitably with the great transition from Scotland to New York City, where, since 1956, I have been a minister at the Madison Avenue Presbyterian Church. I have tried to think through the implications of that change, and its effect on my understanding of the Gospel—how it is to be proclaimed by a Christian community in preaching, worship, and action. I hope there is at least a little flavor of "how my mind has changed" in these reflections on the upheavals through which we have lived in Church and State during these thirty years.

Since I have traveled to many different countries during this period (as I write this I am just off to Yugoslavia with the Appeal of Conscience Foundation), I have had to reckon with the ecumenical dimension of my ministry and what it has meant to me in the "adventure of grace."

This half of my ministry is more difficult to write about because I have had less time to digest what these more recent experiences mean. There is also the added difficulty of the names that are dropped. Most of those I speak about in the first volume are deceased, while most of those mentioned in this book are very much alive. I found it impossible to deal them out of the story, but there are dozens more of whom I could have written who have meant much to me during these years.

I owe more than I can express to the friends in all walks of life, in many different countries, and in all branches of the Church (and in none) who have been to me "angels and ministers of grace." Among these is my invaluable secretary, Carolyn Mathis, who nursed this book to life.

There is one who vetoed mention in the book. Since she is by far the greatest influence, let me skillfully evade the veto by repeating in this introduction the dedication from my book *Virginia Woolf Meets Charlie Brown:*

> TO PAT
> who keeps my feet
> on the ground,
> my mind open,
> and my spirit aloft.

Which is truer than ever.

GRACE
THUS
FAR

Through many dangers, toils and snares,
I have already come;
'Tis grace has brought me safe thus far,
And grace will lead me home.

Chapter One

PICKING UP THE PIECES

When General Patton's Third Army swept past Ziegenhain, which lies between Kassel and Frankfurt, liberating Stalag IXA, we were indeed like those restored to Zion, "like them that dream" (Ps. 126). For a while it was chaos. Prisoners—from America, Britain, France, Russia, and a dozen other lands—were running loose, chiefly in search of food. Until discipline was reimposed, the scene was one of anarchy, and the dream might easily have become a nightmare. The temptation was to break out and raid the neighboring farms and villages. However, the 6th Armored Division, our liberators, soon restored order, and we settled down to await the day we were to be flown home.

I have only scraps of memories of this time—the first few days of freedom after five years as a prisoner. On the heels of the army came a flood of correspondents. It was my first experience with the American press, and they all said the same things. First, "Name and home address?" Then, "Date you were captured?" When I replied "June 12, 1940," the response was always the same: a look of blank incredulity, followed by "Jeeeesus!" Robert Reid, a BBC correspondent, took me aside with a microphone, and I told my tale of the last few days. A week later, having just arrived back in England, I was sitting in a Red Cross café with a crowd of ex-prisoners when the nine o'clock news came on. At the end the newscaster announced, "And now here is an account of the liberation of a stalag," and I found myself listening to my own voice. My name wasn't given, but some old friends recognized me; it was the first news anyone had that I had been liberated. My neighbor in the café turned to me and said, "Who's that?" When I replied "Me," he looked at me as if I were mad.

We were all a little mad. In fact, for some years we P.O.W.s occasionally worried that we had all gone slowly, gracefully 'round the bend. So, whenever new prisoners trickled into our camp after the Normandy invasion with their tales of parachute landings and glider operations, you might hear an elderly colonel of 1940 vintage asking confidentially, "I say, old boy, now that you've settled in, what do you think? Are we really sane?" When I had a spell in our sick bay, I asked the man in the bed next to mine, a young glider pilot, just that question.

"You're really surprisingly normal," he said cheerfully, "except for one thing."

"What's that?" I asked anxiously.

"You don't talk much."

"What do you mean?"

"Well, yesterday I asked someone if there was to be a distribution of parcels in the afternoon. He said 'Yes' and walked away."

"Naturally," I replied. "What else needed to be said?"

"Well, at home, you know, we'd say a lot more, or at least break off with 'I'll be seeing you.' "

"Of all the idiotic things to say," I retorted, and then it dawned on me that we had indeed eliminated all unnecessary conversation. When I got home, the first thing that struck me was the interminable babble of talk—among people waiting in line, people chatting on the street corner, people in restaurants. Yak, yak, yak.

I have other vivid memories of the interim before repatriation. One day I jumped into a small truck I found at the stalag gate and drove at top speed to the nearest village just to prove I hadn't forgotten how to drive. (As a matter of fact, I had, since it was only after I arrived that I realized that the brakes didn't work!) On another occasion I ate and drank through the night with a French Jesuit priest, a missionary, and a couple of doctors. The next day I conducted a burial service for two Americans who had been shot while going through the wire before we had been liberated, and during the course of the service I fainted and had to be hauled out of the grave. Then there was the visit from the burgomaster of the village, who asked the American doctor and me to take charge of dozens of crates of champagne lest the Russians find them. We agreed—and drank nothing else until we were on our way home. There was also a hectic interlude during which I was picked up by an American major who was looking for my former companions at Spangenberg. We drove off to find them and were soon back at the front line, which was not where I wanted to be. Most villages we drove through were decorated with white flags, but occasionally there would be none, whereupon my companion would say, "Keep down, chaplain; this burg hasn't been liberated yet." Eventually we came to my old camp and found a message scribbled in the library to the effect that the prisoners had been marched out three days before. The next night we made contact, and I was given the task of finding food and quarters for my old buddies. So I took over a Luftwaffe airport, then met with the burgomaster, from whom I demanded bread and sausage in huge quantities. It was while I was awaiting the arrival of my old friends, standing on the runway with a young American lieutenant, that I heard a sinister crash, and wondered what it was. I looked down to find the officer lying at my feet. He grinned and said, "You'd better get down, chaplain—that's incoming mail." So my friends had to defend the sumptuous place I had secured for them as the German army made a counterattack, and the major and I made a swift exit via the only remaining open road.

My inglorious military career was rapidly coming to an end. The last job was to lead a column of forty trucks crammed with ex-prisoners across country to the airstrip from whence we were to be flown home. Since I had argued with the American officer in charge about the exact location of the airstrip, he had put me in charge, and was sitting back, smoking and smiling satirically, while I headed the convoy in what I was

5

sure was the right direction. It was, but suddenly in front of us loomed an enormous shell hole. "We'll have to turn around," I thought, and then realized that turning around with forty trucks piled up behind you isn't so easy. In the end I led the whole convoy into a large field and thus skirted the hole.

At the airstrip I was told to send twenty men out each time a plane came in. They were to unload barrels of gasoline and then get in and head home. This operation went on smoothly until sunset, when only I and a sergeant major were left—and no more planes came in. A sympathetic American officer explained that the operation was over for the day and that I could stay overnight with him and proceed home in the morning. I noticed a little cross on his uniform and discovered that he, too, was a chaplain. Soon we were talking theology, the kind that gets modified by war. As it turned out, I made a lifelong friend, for this was Paul Pettit, whom I met again when he studied in Edinburgh and who later, while working for Abingdon Press, published many of my books. It was sad to lose this friend—gentle, thoughtful, humorous, stimulating—in 1983.

The next day I managed to get on a plane. What went through my mind as we crossed the cliffs of Dover and were soon on the ground, being processed and released into a country we hadn't seen for five years? Again it was a kind of dream, not quite real, and I find curious blanks in my memory of the weeks of adjustment. Five years is a big hole out of anyone's life. There was, of course, the enormous excitement of being back home and a deep sense of gratitude to be alive. During confinement, we P.O.W.s never discussed the possibility of not returning, although some of us had serious doubts about the chances of a defeated and desperate Hitler allowing hundreds of thousands of his prisoners to go free.

The only nightmare that I find recurring, however, is not of some massacre but of being in prison for ever and ever—a nightmare shared by others, I have discovered. Yet God had let me come back alive. And so many had died to make that possible. Did it all make any kind of sense? What about this vision of the ministry to which I believed I had been called? Could I re-enter the pulpit and deliver the kind of sermons I

had showered on my prewar congregations? Since I had now
been twice as long in the army as in my first parish, was this
not the time to strike out in another direction? One of my
P.O.W. friends in the regular army even suggested that I stay
on and work in Intelligence. (That had something to do with
my activities in news-gathering and setting up secret radios
in the camps.) Somehow the very suggestion that this was
much more important than chaplaincy work was a sharp reminder of my call to preach. Yes, but what kind of preaching—
and where?

Fortunately, in the midst of all this confusion there was
one clear step ahead. On my leave in 1939, I had been given
charge of the congregation of Greenbank, and they had loyally
accepted an absentee pastor for the duration of the war. They
were waiting to welcome me home. So there I went in the fall
of 1945. There was, however, a difference between moving
from a little country parish to a suburban one in 1939, and
making that same adjustment after six years of war. Was I the
same person, and who were these people to whom I was now
to preach? Picking up the pieces was not going to be easy.

The months before I assumed my pastorate at Greenbank
were a time of bewilderment. It was a nation still at war to
which I returned, and the scars of the bombings left parts of
London unrecognizable. I realized that we were not warriors
returning from enemy territory to the safety and comforts of
home. During the previous five years, for instance, my wife
had worked with the Red Cross through the blitz and then
again through the rocket attacks in 1944, and thus had been
at the receiving end of enemy bombs far more than I had. This
kind of difference in experiences accounted for the fact that,
on the whole, returning prisoners were less violently anti-Ger-
man than those who, for all these years, had never seen a
German except as a prisoner. One of the hideous side effects
of war, I discovered, is the dehumanization of an entire nation.
Civilians believed that the enemy, en masse, was evil, and
therefore anyone in a German uniform was a Nazi villain. But
a prisoner—no matter how much he detested Hitler's regime,
no matter how vigorously he worked to serve the Allied cause
by plotting escapes and by spreading "alarm and despondency"

among the enemy troops—was quite unable to avoid contact with individual Germans who made him realize that the "villain" label was inappropriate. Those familiar with the TV show "Hogan's Heroes" will remember the genial Sergeant Schultz—and there was one in every camp.

My experiences in the camp at Spangenberg brought this lesson home. We were located in the middle of a village and watched the life of the farmers and their families, who showed us no animosity at all—even after the savage bombings of Kassel, which was only ten miles away. One farmer's wife had a charming family whom we watched grow up over the years. Her sweet little girl was a favorite of ours. The woman had some difficulty getting her to return for bedtime, and we used to hear her shout of "Elizabeth!" ringing through the village at night. It was quite common to find about a hundred senior British officers joining in the cry—"Elizabeth! Elizabeth!"—and cheering when she appeared. So it was strange for us to find that back home all Germans were regarded as vicious Nazis. I realized that war makes it possible to hate indiscriminately when the barriers go up and human contact ceases. This is why I believe in maximizing human contacts with nations whose policies we may detest. It is easy to hate an anonymous enemy. It is even easy to hate a Himmler or a Stalin. But it is not easy to hate someone you meet, another human being who shares planet earth with you.

That the war was still on was impressed upon me when I arrived home and remembered a scrap of paper tucked away in my uniform. It contained information given to me after the liberation of our camp by a German officer who was by then our prisoner. I had noted that he had done his best to soften conditions for us in that horrible camp, and when I went to interview him after the liberation, he revealed that he was in the anti-Hitler resistance and had some important information about the whereabouts of certain prominent people whom the Nazis had imprisoned, including Pastor Niemöller. It was important to get this information to the Allied authorities so that these prisoners would not be executed before the liberating army arrived. The officer scribbled down some names and addresses and then, to my surprise, said, "Please get this into the hands of the Bishop of Chichester as soon as you get home." The night I arrived home, I discovered that the Bishop was holding a retreat just around the corner from the house where my wife was staying, and he seemed not at all surprised when I passed along the paper. Within a week I received a note of thanks from the Foreign Office—and thus began a relationship which was to take me back to Germany more than once during the following years. Unfortunately, the camp where Dietrich Bonhoeffer awaited death—some miles to the east of the camp where I was held—was not overtaken until after he had gone to the gallows. I have often wondered why the grace of liberation should have been extended to me while this saint and scholar was hanged before he could be reached. We can be grateful that, through his powerful testimony, "he, being dead, yet speaketh."

It was during those months before I resumed my charge that the momentous things happened. Germany surrendered, then Japan. I have misty recollections of seeing a newspaper headline about the atom bomb. There was, of course, immense relief that the Pacific war was over and that the Allies had been spared the horrors of an invasion of Japan. It seems to me that I sensed only gradually the sinister change that had occurred in our concept of warfare—a change that I had to confront a few years later when I had to present a report to the General Assembly of the Church of Scotland on the doctrine of the "just war" in the light of the discovery and use of the nuclear weapon. I realized that this was something that could not be ignored in the proclamation of the Church. It posed a fearful dilemma for the Christian preacher. (I will have more to say about this later, for, as we all know, the dilemma is still with us, only magnified a thousand times.)

Politics also imposed itself on my thinking at the time through the general election of 1945. During our incarceration, we P.O.W.s had had many discussions about the postwar world we were looking for, and I had read much about the relation between politics and religion. I still have notes from books by such authorities as Archbishop Temple, Reinhold Niebuhr, Christopher Dawson, E. H. Tawney, and others, and I recall

9

plowing through Richard Hooker's *Of the Laws of Ecclesiastical Polity* with unexpected excitement.

Since the result of that election—the removal of Winston Churchill as prime minister—has always been a mystery to people in the United States, my own reactions at the time might be of some interest. Most of us returning prisoners idolized Churchill even more than the country as a whole did. For years he was for us the symbol of ultimate victory, and I used his name constantly in my private propaganda among our guards. (Once, when I was temporarily assigned to a certain stalag, I found our troops plying some guards with tea made from the provisions of our Red Cross parcels. When I mildly scolded them, I was told, "They have to pay for it." When I asked how, the men replied, "Before they drink, they have to raise their arms and say, 'Heil, Churchill.' ") If the general election of 1945 had been the equivalent of a U.S. presidential election, there is no doubt in my mind that Churchill would have been elected by an enormous majority. But it wasn't. The parliamentary system demands that one vote for a local candidate, usually Conservative, Labour, or Liberal. Most of the Conservative candidates seeking our votes were the same people who, as Chamberlain supporters, had kept Churchill out of office for years and had opposed his policies. Now they sought to ride back into Parliament on his coattails, and it seemed to us that they had little in the way of a program to offer. The Labour Party, on the other hand, offered a definite plan for postwar Britain. So I was not in the least surprised when Labour won an overwhelming victory. At the time I felt this party would support our desire for a new start, for a more compassionate approach to the questions of poverty, unemployment, and national health. Like many others, I have since had second thoughts about the wisdom of some of the measures passed by the new government, but the mood of the moment favored change. It used to be said in Britain that if a man didn't vote Socialist when he was thirty, there was something wrong with his heart, and if he didn't vote Conservative when he was fifty, there was something wrong with his head. However that may be, I still believe that our Christian duty is to examine issues on their merits alone, without being slaves to party labels. But the whole question of the grace of God operating in the field of politics must be reserved for another chapter.

Eventually, I was ready to settle in Edinburgh as minister of Greenbank Church, a parish of the Church of Scotland. I was gripped by a sense of responsibility to serve this congregation who had loyally awaited my return. So I was able to resist the siren voices that suggested other avenues of ministry. (Among the more attractive of these was an invitation to assume the editorship of a popular religious weekly.) After all, the years spent in the army were not a total gap in the career of one who had been assured of "grace given" to proclaim "the unsearchable riches of Christ." For during these years I had been conscious of the call to build up the faith of believers and to convert unbelievers. Would I not be answering the same call as I slipped back into the parish routine at home? And was there not a continuity between the pastoral work among the troops and ministering to a suburban congregation in Edinburgh? Frankly, I was not too sure. Was I the same person who had expounded the Scriptures to my rural congregation in Coldstream from 1936 until the outbreak of the war, and was my understanding of those Scriptures and the Christian Gospel still the same? And could I possibly relate to a congregation whose experiences in the last six years had been totally different from mine?

Karl Barth's picture of the preacher as holding the Bible in one hand and the morning newspaper in the other has always appealed to me. It symbolizes the two poles of the preacher's task—one hand, as it were, resting confidently on the eternal Word, the revelation of God's grace in Christ, and the other stretched out sensitively to the here and now, the people and the events to which the preacher must relate. Looking back, I realized that my seminary training had given me a pretty good grip on that Bible, but that my ability to relate it to the events that were really disturbing my flock—whether the sinister news in the papers or their own private distresses—had been somewhat deficient. To put it another way, if it is true that every good sermon either begins in Jerusalem and ends in Manhattan, or begins in Manhattan and ends in Jerusalem, my prewar sermons nearly always began in Jerusalem and seldom reached the High Street of Coldstream.

First I had to think of that Bible. Was my message going to be recognizably the same? I was trying to analyze the effect of five years of more intense biblical and theological study than I had ever done at seminary. That may seem odd, but you have to remember that during my years as a P.O.W. I acquired quite a library of commentaries and religious literature, and had what seemed like unlimited time to devour them. Add to that my omnivorous reading of all kinds of books—in English, French, and German—and it would not be surprising if my thoughts and my beliefs had been shaken up. I'm not suggesting that I spent this interim before returning to Edinburgh in some kind of retreat, neatly sorting out my basic convictions and adjusting my theology. Now there were other things to do—reveling in wandering anywhere I wanted without running into barbed wire and sentry boxes, learning the mysteries of ration books, and enjoying the forgotten sound of the English language spoken by a feminine voice.

The close company of other captured clergy during my imprisonment inevitably put my theology through the mill. With all the normal barriers of politeness down, we argued interminably, especially during the first year or so. Later we reached a point of much greater tolerance of and respect for theological opinions and insights that I would previously have scorned. Equally educational was the opportunity I had, when delivering lectures on the Christian faith, to argue for hours with atheists and agnostics with no holds barred. I learned what arguments had weight and which could be easily shot down, and what the Church really looked like from the outside. Curiously, as a prisoner I experienced a sense of intellectual freedom as I talked about, read, and studied the Bible. I may have felt this way because no ecclesiastical authority was watching over my orthodoxy (not that this had been a problem in the Church of Scotland), or perhaps because I was shaking myself free from the last remnants of my semi-fundamentalist past. Whatever the case, I discovered that the Bible was even more exciting if one didn't feel compelled to find in it the justification for every doctrine and could revel in the sheer humanity of its witness to the divine Word. With an Anglican friend I spent months going through Luke's Gospel, word by word, with the aid of English, French, and German commentaries I had acquired by various means in different camps.

One scene comes back to me. We chaplains and doctors who had been expecting repatriation had been sent to a stalag in Silesia in the depths of winter. Our hut was like a refrigerator day and night, and in the evenings we huddled around one little stove, swathed up to our eyebrows in every article of clothing we owned. My friend and I decided that, despite the conditions, we would continue our study of Luke. One night we were studying a difficult passage about the Holy Spirit, and I was trying to recall my vanishing Hebrew to explain Luke's Greek. Suddenly a voice behind us said in broken English, "Perhaps I can help." I turned and saw a shaggy figure in a filthy uniform. He had been captured while working for the British army in a port in the Middle East. In a few minutes he gave us a fascinating lecture on the Hebrew words that are translated "spirit" in English. Eventually I asked him where he had acquired his knowledge, and he replied offhandedly, "Oh, I was an assistant to Professor Kittel" (the most famous biblical linguistic scholar in the world).

Looking back on these theological and biblical adventures as I prepared to resume a normal ministry at home, I realized that nothing in my basic convictions about the Christian Gospel had changed. I was still sure that I had been called to "proclaim the unsearchable riches of Christ." But I had discovered that these riches were indeed "unsearchable," and I was now prepared to believe that I had much more searching to do. Once, when I felt that death was imminent, I remember that instant of winnowing in which my fundamental beliefs were separated from the rest. Actually, my entire P.O.W. experience was a winnowing process. It made me realize that I might be less certain about some peripheral doctrines, but that the Christ who had been through every trial we can possibly know was more real to me than ever, and his victory was indeed God's victory, and could be mine. In my understanding of the Church I had become more catholic in the sense in which we use the term in the creeds—"I believe in the holy catholic

Church." My reading in theology ranging across the centuries, my New Testament studies, my close contact with believers of very diverse traditions, my increasing respect for the enduring testimony in worship and service to the apostolic Gospel—all combined to enlarge my vision of the one, holy, catholic, and apostolic Church in which we Presbyterians historically find our place.

At the same time, I discovered that I had not ceased to be evangelical in the sense of seeking to spread the Gospel and "making disciples." My adventures in interpreting the Gospel to fellow prisoners and my reading of the masterminds of evangelism, from Augustine and Wesley to C. S. Lewis, had nourished my hope to use such talents as I had to interpret the Gospel to a new generation. At the same time, my experiences in the camps had made me much less ready to decide who was a Christian and who wasn't. It was disturbing at first to discover that a genial, down-to-earth, no-nonsense character with no apparent piety or churchmanship often acted in a much more Christian way when it came to sharing food in times of privation than another who made a big fuss about his Christian convictions. In fact, what you might call "high-pressure religion"—whether of the extreme fundamentalist or the High Church variety—was not productive of selflessness and generosity when it came to practical tests. I began to realize that an intense concern for the salvation of one's soul is often accompanied by an equally intense desire to secure the needs of the body.

So I still had a Gospel to preach, and a Gospel less rigid in its form and more inclusive in its application than in my previous understanding. I could still be the preacher with the Bible in one hand. But what about the other? This was a far more difficult adjustment. I had become convinced that the morning newspaper (meaning the events of the day and the people to whom the preacher speaks) was as important as the explication of Scripture. Looking back, I realized that in my first parish I had been greatly concerned that my message be a faithful exposition of the Bible, but had not been equally sensitive to the real needs and concerns of my flock. I had assumed that a local shopkeeper or farm laborer would be as thrilled to hear what Amos had to say to Amaziah, the priest of Bethel, as we seminarians had been. It had taken a traumatic event on the national level—like the Munich Agreement—to bring a current moral-political issue into my sermons. The prison camps had taught me an unforgettable lesson in communication. Preaching there meant preaching to a congregation whom I knew more intimately than any group of people I have known before or since. There was no barrier whatever between pulpit and pew. We spoke the same language; we shared the same worries; we ate the same food; we knew one another as well as husband and wife. It was not possible to follow any double standard; it was not like being at home, where a preacher could deliver an eloquent sermon on Christian love and then go home and kick the dog. Comment after the sermon was not confined to compliments. (I remember a colonel with a taste for sermons saying one Sunday, "Interesting sermon, David, but what was the point of it?") In other words, I was forced to communicate honestly—or there would be no congregation at all.

Now the question was, How could I communicate with a people whose life and experiences had now become strange to me? My first attempts to preach at Greenbank did not present this problem acutely because the congregation was, like everyone else, eager to hear endless illustrations drawn from the prison experience, but I soon began to realize that we were speaking a different language. Over these five years we prisoners had developed a language of our own. I remember looking around a bookshop with my wife and seeing a novel entitled *Goon in the Block*. I immediately bought it, and my wife asked, "What on earth does that phrase mean?" To me, "goon in the block" was an everyday shout warning the inhabitants of a prison block who might be busy with some escape plans that a "goon"—our name for a German guard—was sniffing around.

There was one immediate problem for a returned clergyman like me: over the years I had forgotten which words were acceptable in respectable mixed company and which were not. It took me a little time to negotiate that hurdle. Even if I managed to avoid certain four-letter words in my sermons, it was evident that a large gulf of misunderstanding separated me from my parishioners. I might make a remark I thought was funny and get no response, or I might say something that I considered perfectly normal and be greeted by a burst of laughter. It may not have been too noticeable to my very tolerant congregation, but there were times when I felt the frustration of this language barrier. Eventually, of course, I reassimilated the conventions of civilian speech. But even then a question hovered in the back of my mind: Am I really talking the language of ordinary people, or am I just making the kind of noises that are expected of a preacher talking to "churchy" people? That question haunts me still.

Something happened early on that was an enormous help to me in this process of picking up the pieces. I felt drawn to the teenagers in my congregation because they were more open to unconventional approaches to religion and responsive to the direct and "non-churchy" language to which I had become accustomed. The "Bible class" the church offered didn't draw very many of them, and it occurred to me that a large number of them might be attracted by a different approach. So I announced a new activity called "Quest"—the word I had chosen for my lectures in Spangenberg—and invited any teens between the ages of fourteen and eighteen to meet me after the evening service. About twenty turned up, and we had a lively time discussing the topics they brought up. I found it much easier to communicate with them than with the adults. Within a few months the group had over a hundred members, and I divided it into junior and senior sections. We talked openly, and I soon learned what was on their minds—and what wasn't. After weeks of free discussion, what I was hoping for happened. They came to me and said something like this: "We're tired of hearing our opinions on all these topics. We want to know how the Christian faith speaks and what it means. Will you give us a series of lectures on doctrine?" From that they went on to study other religions and political parties (including the Communist Party), and branched out into various social projects, ranging from presenting satirical musicals to visiting the local homes for the aged. From all I hear, "Quest" is still alive and well at Greenbank.

My passion for travel had not been quenched by my war-

time experience of being shuttled around Germany from time
to time under somewhat primitive conditions. (I love trains,
but traveling on one as a prisoner meant falling very low on
the priority list of creature comfort. I remember two days and
two nights between Rouen and Lamsdorf when I was lucky
enough to secure a seat in the lavatory, and spent hours reading the Russian Orthodox theology of Nicolas Berdyaev, despite innumerable necessary interruptions.) I was also anxious
to be active in what was called "interchurch relations," foster-
ing the newly born ecumenical movement. Thus I was delighted when the Bishop of Chichester asked me to represent
the Church of Scotland in a delegation of British church leaders
seeking to renew contact with our German neighbors. I have
to confess that it was not altogether unacceptable to travel
around Germany as a V.I.P., with the temporary rank of
colonel—and, to the surprise of my companions, to find in
every area ex-P.O.W. friends in helpful positions of authority.
But the scenes of devastation and the immediate needs of the
people—it was just a year since the war had ended—were
unforgettable.

Our tour made possible the first personal contact between
British and German Christians, and we rejoiced that such a
thing could happen so soon. It was deeply moving to visit
Herford, where the congregation overflowed from the cathedral
and packed the square outside. The word had gone around that
the Bishop of Chichester was going to preach, and the people
were ready to hang on his every word. Never before or since
have I heard "Ein' feste Burg" sung with such tremendous
power and conviction. Another memorable occasion was an
ecumenical service in the Gedächtniskirche in Berlin. It had
been heavily bombed, and the cold autumn wind whistled
through the walls as we processed up the aisle. The car that
contained all our luggage and robes had been stolen on our
way to Berlin, so we were not warmly dressed. Suddenly, I
recognized the figure beside me: it was Martin Niemöller.
When we returned to the robing room after the service, I wanted
to talk with him. I wondered just what kind of man he was,
and the first cue was not long in coming. Since the first thing
he did after disrobing was to throw himself into a chair and

light up a pipe, I knew that communication was going to be easy. We talked about the Nazi period, about his arrest and imprisonment, about his release, and about the future of Europe and the role of the Church in the period of reconstruction. At one point I asked him if he had visited Scotland. He grinned and said, "I cruised in the Firth of Forth in 1915," and I was reminded of his activities as a U-boat commander in World War I.

During these early postwar years, I made many other contacts with the churches in Europe, and I attended the meeting of the Alliance of Reformed Churches in Geneva in 1948. There I met some old friends from France and Switzerland and made new ones from Czechoslovakia, Hungary, and Holland. Professor Hromadka from Prague was there. He was a controversial figure at the time because he had lent some support to the Communist coup. He told me how he owed his faith to Dr. David Cairns of Aberdeen, who had helped him through a difficult period in his seminary days. He also explained that he believed that some kind of revolution had been necessary in Czechoslovakia, but that he thought the Church could survive and be effective under the new regime. I remember his saying, "The time has not yet come to say No, but when it does, I will speak out." I waited for that time, and indeed, shortly before he died, Hromadka published an open letter to Brezhnev protesting the invasion of Czechoslovakia by Soviet troops in 1968.

One Sunday morning I was surprised to see Rudolf Bultmann in the congregation. Bultmann was professor of New Testament at Marburg University. For a time he had been associated with Barth, but he had become famous in theological circles through his attempt to carry out a radical program of what he called "demythologizing" the New Testament. His attack on the historicity of much of the material in the Gospels made him a *bête noire* in orthodox circles.

His being there triggered a memory. In 1944, at the height of the invasion battles, a curious thing had happened to me. A high-ranking German officer had appeared in our camp and announced that he hoped to improve conditions for British officers in captivity. He was received with some skepticism, even derision, as he solemnly handed out sheets of paper on which we were invited to offer suggestions for making our life more tolerable. All kinds of suggestions flowed in—some sensible, some ludicrous, some satirical, some scathing. (I remember one officer asking someone to tell him how to spell "atrocity.") Among my own list of suggestions I included the following: "As a former student at Marburg University, I would like to pay a visit there." Six weeks later I was summoned by the British senior officer. "Do you remember the good-relations officer and our requests?" he asked. "About the only one they have agreed to is your idiotic request to visit Marburg." So it came about that, at the height of the war in the West, I set off for Marburg, traveling in comfort by train with a German officer and a corporal. I insisted on going first-class. We were received by the president of the University, who made a formal speech and asked if I had any special request. Remembering in time that such a dignitary was entitled to be addressed as "Magnifizenz," I replied in kind and asked if I could see Professor Bultmann. "Nicht möglich" (not possible) was the answer. Could I attend a theological lecture? "Nicht möglich." Or buy some books? "Nicht möglich." Perhaps borrow some books from the library? "Ya," he said, and departed. Thus I acquired two volumes of Calvin's *Institutes* to take back to the camp. I managed to rescue them in the confusion at the end of the war, and even to restore them eventually to Marburg.

Well, there was Bultmann in my congregation, the guest of a New College professor. The professor entertained us both at lunch, and I asked Bultmann if he knew of my wartime attempt to see him. He said he had known about it, but he also knew that because he was a suspect character there was no hope of his being allowed to see me. A year or so later I was visiting German churches and seminaries under the auspices of the Foreign Office and was due to lecture to the Reformed churches in the Wuppertal/Barmen area. I took a detour by the Marburg Library and rang up Bultmann. "I'd say, 'Come to dinner,' " he responded, "but as my wife's away, it will have to be for a bowl of spaghetti." So I spent a fascinating evening eating "spaghetti à la Bultmann" and learning firsthand what he was after with the demythologizing. To my surprise, he described his intentions as evangelistic. Like me, he was deeply concerned with the communication of God's message and was trying to rephrase the Gospel in terms acceptable to the modern mind. Unlike me, he seemed prepared to surrender the supernatural. Theologically this was an unequal contest, of course, but I left with a deeper understanding of his existentialist interpretation of the Gospel. Upon arriving in Barmen, the heart of Reformed theology (the Barmen Declaration was the Barthian counterblast to the Nazi pretensions), I horrified my hosts by telling them where I had been. I calmed them by assuring them that I was thoroughly "de-Bultmannized."

One of the pieces to be picked up was my reintegration into the Presbyterian system, with its courts and committees. It was at this point that I realized that, although loyal to my ordination vows of subjection to Presbytery, Synod, and General Assembly, and increasingly interested in the politics of Church and State, I was in no way attracted to the sphere of church politics and legalities. I was (and am) grateful that some ministers delight in matters of administration and the running of the ecclesiastical machine, but my interests and such skills as I had lay elsewhere. One way of putting it was that I had no moderatorial ambitions—despite the fact that a camp artist at Spangenberg had done a devastating cartoon of me that he labeled "Moderator Read, circa 1965."

Writing was exercising its spell on me, and I was soon engaged in composing *The Christian Faith* for Hodder and Stoughton's "Teach Yourself" series. (The book was subsequently published in America in both hardback and paperback.) Len Cutts, my publisher friend, was on my trail, and one day he came to make me a special proposition. "I feel that you have one big book inside you," he said, "and I want you to think about writing it. Take your time—five years or even ten." At that moment my wife entered the room, and her first words were, "If you've come to get a book out of David, tell him you must have it next month." And the truth is that I have never been able to write at leisure. (Indeed, this book is being written during the very busiest period of my year.) So Cutts went away, disappointed, but remained a wonderful friend and advisor on the books I subsequently wrote.

Broadcasting was another attraction. Radio seemed to me God-given for communicating with an entire nation in the privacy of their homes, and I wanted to learn how to do it. Ronnie Falconer, the head of the Scottish BBC's religious department, got me to broadcast from the church and do other series of studio talks. He was a devoted churchman, expert in his chosen field, and yet very much aware of the dangers of such a thing as a "radio church." He saw broadcasting as an ally of the local parish church and as an instrument that evangelism could use to soften the opposition. Eventually he groomed me for the initial efforts at religious television.

Theology continued to hold a special fascination for me. I was fortunate to be within traveling distance of New College, with its galaxy of scholars who were wonderfully accessible. As I look back now, it seems amazing that I should have found myself in a Bible study group run by William Manson and including such people as Matthew Black, John Baillie, Tom Torrance, J. K. S. Reid, and other world-renowned writers. Was this the direction in which I should go? The question became pressing when I was asked to accept the nomination for a chair in theology. Was this what God's grace had in store for me? Or was I running away from the voice that had said, "Go thou and preach"? My parish won out. After all, there was not only the preaching but the pastoral work that made preaching possible. I needed to know people, who are the raw material of theology, and to bring them in a personal way the consolations of the Gospel.

Not all, of course, were anxious for such consolations. One day my wife met a somewhat inactive church member who informed her that her husband was ill.

"Would he like a visit from Mr. Read?" my wife asked.

"Oh, no," was the reply. "He's not as bad as that."

Chapter Two

WHAT KIND
OF
A PREACHER?

As I slipped into the routine of the Scottish parish minister and gradually adjusted to normal civilian ways, several questions kept haunting me. Was church life simply resuming where it had left off in 1939, as if the war years had been merely an unfortunate interlude? Just as, during the prison years, we P.O.W.s had found it hard to conceive that life at home—despite some privations, alarms, and excursions—was going on as usual, so many of us expected much greater changes in postwar Britain than we found. There was something vaguely depressing about the familiarity of everyday life, especially in a city like Edinburgh, which had been spared any major air raids, and which, in any case, has a tendency to settle back contentedly into its well-defined ruts. (To this day, when I return and run into some old friend, I am seldom asked questions about life in the United States. The usual remark is, "Well, you'll be glad to get back.")

Was it really possible that the global upheaval, the huge numbers of casualties, the Holocaust (about which we were gradually learning the almost unbelievable facts), the new threats that were looming as we became aware of Communist expansion, and the invention and use of the atomic bomb—that all this could have had little or no effect on the outlook—in particular, the religious beliefs—of the average man and woman? Could the message and the methods of the Church really be unaffected by all that had happened during these catastrophic years? Older people remembered that World War I had shattered many illusions of the previous era—especially the calm assumption that the world was on an escalator of scientific and moral progress leading inevitably to a utopia of prosperity and peace which church people were only too ready to identify with the Kingdom of God. There was a reaction of cynicism and disillusionment which had left the churches of Western Europe in the weakest position they had been in for centuries, a decline from which they have not yet recovered. Was there to be no detectable reaction at all after this second global convulsion?

When I was asked to speak during Holy Week of 1945 in a large West End church, I discussed with the minister what my topic would be. I remember spelling out some of these questions that had been on my mind. To my surprise, he pounced on one and suggested that it be my subject. What I had said, almost inadvertently, was that I thought people might be wondering what was left of Christianity. "That," he said, "is your topic." I don't remember exactly what I said when I spoke, but I know that I said something about the new world that was being shaped in these postwar years and how the Church was to speak to it and act in it as the Body of Christ on earth.

There were, of course, some prophetic voices heard and new movements spawned which gave grounds for hope that the churches were not simply seeking a return to the status quo before 1939. The Iona Community, under the leadership of George MacLeod, was one. In the thirties George had the vision of combining a restoration of the old abbey at Iona with an attempt to again relate the Church to the employed—and unemployed—in areas like his own parish of Govan on the Clyde. The community brought together ministers, seminarians, and artisans who worked physically at the rebuilding, and labored mentally and spiritually in worship and discussion groups. The community (with its "associates," of which I was one) had many facets. For some it brought the Church into the political arena—which they either approved of or dis-

liked. For others it represented a revival of worship that was
both catholic and vigorously contemporary. Some welcomed
a movement that was free to respond to the new world without
being crippled by the machinery of the organized Church,
while others were anxious to see the community properly subject to Presbyterian polity. Still others were attracted by the
emphasis on prayer and Bible study. The fact that the community was clearly a catalyst for controversy was attractive to
me during this period. Much of the furor centered on the per-
sonality of George MacLeod, and this seems a good point at
which to pay tribute to one who had a great influence on
preachers of my vintage. As one who has argued with him for
fifty years in public and in private, I think of him not only
with deep affection but with admiration and gratitude. For me,
he was, along with less unconventional preachers like James S.
Stewart, what it is now fashionable to call a "role model."

There were also preachers who were deeply concerned
about our devotional life and organized retreats at which we
sought a form of piety (in the true sense of the word) that drew
on the historic treasures of the Church but was also alert to
the new age. Presbyterians, who are too fond of talking, have
never been very good at this kind of thing. I confess that my
experience of retreats at this time was less fruitful than it might
have been, since being boxed up somewhere with other ministers, subject to a fixed routine, and having to deal with extended periods of silence reminded me too painfully of a P.O.W.
camp. Still, I realized that something was missing in the devotional life of most of us preachers that these retreats attempted to nurture into existence. About the only part of Bishop
Robinson's best-selling *Honest to God* that brought an "amen"
from me was the section in which he talked about the "dead
shelf" in a minister's library where repose the innumerable
little books one has acquired in the hope that they will revo-
lutionize one's private prayers.

In the late forties the Church began to face again the question of evangelism. It was obvious that large segments of the
population were almost entirely divorced from the Church and
ignorant of its teachings or even of its purpose. Prior to the
war, the Church Extension movement had done much to pro-

vide new churches for the new towns that were springing up then, but there was clearly a need for the national Church to reach out with a vigorous affirmation of the Gospel in terms that could be understood by those who were being described at the time as "the new pagans." I joined a group that set in motion a nationwide mission under the title "Tell Scotland." With vigorous help from the religious department of the BBC, the campaign had a considerable impact, although it could hardly be said that the whole nation waited breathlessly to discover what we had to tell.

I remember that at this point I was still convinced that my calling as a preacher included the call to be an evangelist. I was seeking an evangelism that tried humbly to understand what it was that prevented many of our contemporaries, including our close friends, from responding to the Gospel of Christ. Many of us had managed to retain the conviction that the Church lives by spreading the Good News and that it is a vital part of the preacher's task to "make disciples" according to the command of Jesus, while at the same time rejecting the popular notion of evangelism as an arrogant and intrusive attempt to bludgeon the unbeliever into submission. How can we proclaim the Gospel, publicly or privately, without seeming to insist on imposing *our* beliefs as superior to any others? With the help of writers like C. S. Lewis, and a rereading of G. K. Chesterton (with his Roman polemics strained out), I realized that I had indeed been doing the work of an evangelist in the P.O.W. camps—so long as I avoided the topic of "my religion" and relayed the New Testament witness to Christ. As the Fourth Gospel says of John the Baptist, "He was not that light but was sent to bear witness to the light"—an excellent text to have inscribed on every pulpit where the preacher can see it.

There was still the question—and it's with us today—of finding the words and actions to convey the Christian story to those for whom conventional "churchy" language and liturgy is so much gobbledygook.

About this time I was invited to deliver the Warrack Lectures on preaching, the Scottish equivalent of the Lyman Beecher Lectures at Yale. I decided to renounce yet one more investigation of the nature of the sermon—to offer no advice on how to construct a model sermon, properly outlined and brilliantly illustrated—but to address the question of what I called "The Communication of the Gospel." Later these lectures appeared in print under that title. Since I am allergic to reading anything I have written—even last week's sermon, let alone a book published over thirty years ago—I can't summarize any great thoughts I may have had. But shortly after the lectures were published, I had an experience that brought home to me the need to be cautious in making generalizations about what liberal theologians used to call "the modern mind," and that taught me that evangelists come in all theological shapes and cultural sizes. On a visit to London I went to Harringay to hear an American evangelist called Billy Graham.

Aware that I had committed myself to the view that the day of the old-fashioned mass meeting—with its hearty singing, dramatic use of the Bible, and appeal for decisions—was over, I sat spellbound while this young man spoke to a huge crowd who were by no means nostalgic churchgoers looking for a new Moody and Sankey. Aware that in *The Communication of the Gospel* I had spent pages pleading for a new, fresh vocabulary with which to relay the New Testament message, I found myself listening to every well-worn cliché in the traditional evangelistic vocabulary, and—damn it—this contemporary crowd was hanging on every word. This man communicated much more effectively than I could. And the result—the procession of inquirers who responded to the appeal—was not what is so often caricatured. These people came forward quietly and solemnly, rather like Anglicans receiving Holy Communion. God has given Billy the gift of communication, a gift of the Spirit, not of well-researched techniques, and that, along with his transparent sincerity, was the secret. So it was that a few years later I invited him to speak to the students at Edinburgh University, and still later encouraged my New York parish to support the Billy Graham Crusade of 1956. It's not that I believe this method to be the fulfillment of our evangelistic task. (In fact, in the hands of some later practitioners, it has become one of the greatest obstacles to a real communication of the Gospel.) Nor do I always hear what Billy is hearing when he declares "The Bible says. . . ." But he has taught me that there is more than one way of communicating, and I admire the way he has in recent days avoided aligning himself with the sinister marriage of extreme fundamentalism and extreme right-wing politics.

What kind of a preacher am I? Yes, the urge to interpret the Gospel to the unbeliever is still with me, all the more urgently as we pass through this dangerous period when the average citizen seems often to be confronted with a false choice in religion—either to remain genially agnostic or to succumb to the blandishments of the fanatics.

But other aspects of the preacher's call were pressing on me at this time. In my seminary days I had learned from both professors and fellow students that preaching is not something that happens in a vacuum, and that it is not exclusively directed at converting the sinner. In my first parish and during my years as a P.O.W., I came to understand more of the way in which a sermon functions to build up the faith of a congregation. It's a pity we can't use the word "edification" without being misunderstood, for this is exactly what sermons, from New Testament times onward, have most surely been providing. In Nazi Germany it was the churches that had been nourished in biblical faith that stood firm when the crisis came. If critical times should come for us in this country, it is churches that have been literally "edified" in the faith that will count, and not those that have depended solely on charismatic personalities or fireworks in the pulpit. I learned in the camps and at Greenbank that few church members have received much religious instruction through lectures or private study, and so I began to think more about both the educational task and the integration of the sermon into the worship of the Church.

There were scholars around who had much to teach me about such things as preaching doctrine and the importance of the liturgy. I learned, for instance, that liturgy is not something you either have or don't have in a service. You either have a good liturgy or a bad one. (While I make no claim for perfection for our Service Book at Madison Avenue, you should see some of the bulletins that come across my desk.) What kind of a preacher was I becoming? At least one who had disentangled himself from the notion that people should come at eleven o'clock on a Sunday morning to "hear Dr. So-and-so," before which supreme moment they must endure what in the bad old days in Scotland were known as "the preliminaries." When I left Greenbank, it pleased me to have a parishioner say that during my tenure she had learned to worship; I was happy that she had not merely complimented me on my sermons. Similarly, I was delighted when someone at Madison Avenue once remarked that, when we shifted the sermon from the end to the middle of the service, he had learned what worship really means.

All this meant a continual shaking up of my call to be a preacher, and of course there was always that temptation to strike out in another direction: to join a community that was breaking out of the parish pattern, to become a full-time evangelist with an eye on radio and television, to get into the ecumenical movement at the organizational level, to work with the Student Christian Movement (which at that time was in its most biblical and evangelical mood), or to succumb to the appeal of theology and become a seminary professor. I wasn't given to fits of introspection. Nor did I in my prayers attempt to persuade the Lord that I could really serve him better in one of these directions. I didn't even make any moves to clear the way for a change. It has always seemed to me that it is God who makes the moves, sometimes in strange ways and through unexpected people.

About this time I was becoming aware of an issue in the life of the Church from which I had been partly shielded during my army chaplaincy: the highly controversial matter of the relationship between Church and State—or, as some like to put it, politics and religion. I had been raised in a family in which political questions were constantly discussed, and had been exposed to books and lectures on the political process from the days of the ancient Athenians. I had grown accustomed to arguing with my father when our views began to differ. I was also by this time acquainted with numerous members of Parliament from different parties. So it is not surprising that these postwar years led me to think pretty rigorously about the role of the Church in national and international affairs. Thus it was that I readily accepted an invitation to become a member of the Church and Nation Committee of the General Assembly. Taking this position was an illuminating experience. It was the task of this committee to review all questions in the political arena which had ethical implications and, therefore, on which the Church might be expected to make pronouncements in the light of the Gospel. We compiled and delivered a report to the General Assembly, which debated it and approved certain deliverances as the unanimous or majority view of that body. Presbyterians in the United States are familiar with this process, but there are features of the Scottish situation that are very different from the American in questions of Church and State. A word about them might help to explain certain biases some have claimed to detect in my views on current controversies in the United States.

The Church of Scotland is by law established, but the Scottish establishment is historically unique. It simply means that the Presbyterian Church is recognized by the State as the national Church, and the first act of a monarch of Great Britain on her or his accession is to swear to maintain Presbyterian Church government in Scotland. But, unlike other religious establishments such as that in England, the Church of Scotland has total freedom in its government and doctrines and ways of worship. Thanks to those like David Haxton (with whom I began this "theobiography") who fought for the spiritual independence of the Church, neither monarch nor Parliament has any jurisdiction in the Church, nor does the Church receive financial support of any kind from the state. What this establishment does is to offer a public forum for the voice of the Church that still attracts considerable attention. The proceedings of the General Assembly held each year in Edinburgh are front-page news in the papers, and its deliverances are debated by the media. The meetings of the Assembly are presided over by the Moderator, who subsequently represents the Church with regular access to what some like to call "the corridors of power," and who, on all official occasions in Scotland, ranks only after the monarch and the Lord High Chancellor. The Assembly is always attended either by the monarch or by a Lord

High Commissioner (who lives in the palace of Holyrood House and is received as royalty for the duration of his or her term of office). However, neither the monarch nor the Commissioner may set foot on the floor of the Assembly—a symbol of the Church's independence.

All this sounds rather horrifying to American ears, and I have no intention of defending the practice of religious establishment, which is vanishing from almost every country today. Let me just say that it has certain advantages, especially when a nation has very few other religions and has a big majority who would at least claim to be Presbyterians. It is an establishment of a much more onerous—not to say oppressive— nature that was expressly forbidden by the First Amendment of the American Constitution. As I shall later describe, it was a cultural shock for me to leave a parish in Edinburgh (and the word "parish" in the vocabulary of a national church means a body of worshipers that includes every family that resides in a particular area), where about ninety percent were Presbyterians, and become a minister in New York City, where all the Protestants put together are barely one-tenth of the population, and few have the slightest idea of what a General Assembly does or says. I welcome the fact that ministry here carries no whiff of the prestige of an establishment, that a preacher is not usually expected to echo the views of government, nor the worship of the Church to be seen, as the saying goes, as "the Conservative Party at prayer." It is good that the Presbyterian Church has no special position in the State—and, of course, even better that no other denomination does! I can't help pointing out, however, that the famous amendment says nothing about a wall of separation between Church and State, and I confess that it has been hard for me to follow the logic whereby all kinds of rules have been extrapolated from the one plain rejection of any particular religious establishment.

My Church of Scotland background, then, has inoculated me with the conviction that the Church has a mission to address those public issues that clearly contain ethical judgments, and that the preacher is not to be solely concerned with nurturing a private piety in his flock. At the same time, this tradition has bred in me a belief that the Church must be both

31

restrained and informed in its excursions into the political fields, and that the preacher must normally refrain completely from taking sides in party politics and advocating support for particular candidates. In the late forties the Church and Nation Committee of the General Assembly was plunged into questions ranging from the hydrogen bomb to the Sunday opening of movie theatres. It was an education for me to hear ministers and elders with political views ranging from strong left to strong right, church men and women—including trade unionists, employers, journalists, aristocrats—all tackling these thorny questions with no holds barred.

One of the great debates for which the Assembly is famous took place over a deliverance of the Church and Nation Committee giving reluctant support to the government's decision to develop the hydrogen bomb. It was proposed by James Pitt-Watson, chairman of the Committee, and vigorously opposed by George MacLeod. Although the latter's radical pacifist stance has never been the majority position of the Church of Scotland, the opposition was defeated by the eloquent and passionate debate that engaged the conscience of all present. Cabinet ministers in the Visitors' Gallery were heard to compare the level of debate favorably with that in the House of Commons. The dilemma for Christians came through loud and clear. Those who went along with the armaments proposal had to face the possibility of another and much more terrible Hiroshima; those who rejected all military defense against a totalitarian power had to reckon with exposing our people to an Auschwitz. The dilemma is still with us. The temptation for the Church, then and now, is to try to avoid facing the consequences of either the pacifist or the nonpacifist position. Pacifists, it seems to me, must recognize the appalling dangers to which they would expose others if such a view were to prevail. On the other hand, those whose Christian conscience allows for armaments for defense must face the question of how much weaponry is necessary. The Church in Britain and in the United States played, on the whole, a feeble and dangerous role in the 1930s by saying in effect that it was all right to have armaments but then opposing any effort to amass sufficient weapons to successfully counter the Nazi threat.

Soon after the report of the Church and Nation Committee was debated, I was asked to chair an Assembly committee on the subject of "the just war." The "just war" doctrine has been the classic position, first elaborated by Saint Augustine, of both Catholic and Protestant churches (except for those committed to a pacifist theology), and it has recently surfaced in the discussion arising out of the Catholic bishops' letter on the use of nuclear weapons. In essence, this doctrine states that it is legitimate for Christians to resort to force provided that there is a "just cause" and that war is waged by "just means" (which means, among other things, limiting the devastating power of the weapons used and avoiding civilian casualties). After a rather unsatisfactory series of discussions, mostly on the pacifist issue, we produced a report which said that while it was still possible in the nuclear age to wage a war for a just cause, it was no longer possible to use just means. Although I received a kind letter from Reinhold Niebuhr, to whom I sent a copy of the report, I must admit that it was not a very helpful statement—but then, what would be?

A few years later, while at a dinner, I overheard a Moderator denouncing the report. Catching my eye, and not knowing that I had had anything to do with it, he asked, "Don't you agree, David?"

"To a great extent I do," I replied. "You see, I wrote it."

These political forays were, of course, expanding my horizons as a preacher. And so were various ecumenical journeys I took during these years. In 1948 I attended the conference of the World Alliance of Reformed Churches at Geneva, where I had my first experience of the theological liveliness and administrative vigor of American Presbyterianism. I remember particularly a brilliant address on our liturgical tradition by a young Texan named James McCord. We had morning prayers in Calvin's chapel, and one morning I overheard an American voice in the pew behind me asking that great ecclesiastical statesman, John Mackay, if he knew of a Scotsman named David Read. It was then that I was introduced to Harrison Ray Anderson of Chicago, who had heard me preach at St. Giles' the previous week. He proceeded to invite me to go on a preaching and lecturing tour of the United States. It never

33

occurred to me at the time that this was the first link in a chain of events that was to lead me to a new country and to a church where I would preach for thirty years. It was appropriate that this prevenient grace should be at work right there in Calvin's chapel.

The following year I presided at the first World Presbyterian Youth Conference, which was held at my former seminary in Montpellier in the south of France. It was thrilling to be with the younger generation and to try to be the interpreter not only of the three languages that were being spoken but of the ecumenical dimensions of the Reformed family. For my own Scottish contingent, it was enlightening to hear the French and Germans discussing their wartime experiences and the role of the Church in the new age. We also had delegates from Africa, one of whom taught us a hymn from his native Ghana which became the theme song for the conference.

In 1947 came another mysterious invitation—to preach at the parish church of Crathie, which the royal family attended, and spend the weekend at Balmoral Castle as I had in 1939. All I remember about the sermon this time was that my theme was the transfiguration of Jesus, and that I used a risky illustration to show how a scientific description of an event is not necessarily the most true. "If you heard the world's greatest violinist playing," I said, "you could describe what was happening in terms of beauty and ecstasy—or else you could say, quite accurately, that you were watching a man drawing some horses' hair over the guts of a cat." This provoked an explosion of laughter from the royal pew, an outburst led by Princess Margaret, who afterwards explained to me the private joke that touched off the whole family. At that time, Princess Elizabeth (now the Queen) and Prince Philip were engaged, and the Queen (now the Queen Mother) presided over a rollicking weekend with her unfailing charm and kindness. The King was good enough to invite me to drive over with him to see the Duchess of Kent, and it was fun to watch the reactions of those we passed on the road when they saw who was at the wheel. This is the point at which to stop these happy recollections, for there floats into my mind a remark attributed to a former chaplain to the Queen: "If there's anything the Queen and I dislike, it's name-dropping."

Where, then, was I going as a preacher and pastor? I enjoyed Greenbank and its people, and Edinburgh had shaken off its stuffiness to the extent of launching a Festival of the Arts—which everyone said would fail because it was too soon after the war, and anyway, the Edinburgh weather would doom it from the start. But the predictions proved wrong. The weather, usually fickle, rewarded us all by providing three weeks of blazing sunshine and temperatures in the seventies. The shortages of food and drink did little to dampen the spirits of our visitors. My wife and I joined others in providing coffee and cakes in our manse to visiting celebrities every evening at about midnight.

I was not spending any time with the question, What next? Every time some thought occurred to me about fulfilling another role in the communication of the Gospel, the pulpit kept pulling me back. At Greenbank we now had over twelve hundred members on the rolls, so there was plenty to do besides preparing sermons. It seems incredible to me now, but for ministering to the needs of a congregation of this size we had no assistants, no secretaries, no office, and no mimeograph machine, let alone a computer! To put it bluntly, the full-time paid staff consisted of the minister and the beadle. A beadle, I should explain to the uninitiated, is the man employed to look after the property and assist the minister in a hundred subtle ways (such as covering up for a forgetful pastor when he doesn't show up for an engagement, providing tactful information about "difficult" members, and helping to trace the minister's car when he has forgotten outside which house he has left it). Beadles are also famous for their repartee and observations on church life. Many years ago, at a big West End church in Edinburgh, it was decided to keep the doors open during the week. The beadle disapproved. When he was asked by an elder if many people came into the church on weekdays to pray, his reply was, "Aye, I've catched one or two of them at it." My own beadle was a gem, with a poker face and an irrepressible sense of humor. At one time we had an American seminarian helping in the church (unpaid!) who delighted everyone by getting engaged to the leader of our "Quest" group. This was at a time when, owing to a dollar shortage, many goods in the shops were affordable only to foreign—especially American—visitors. One Sunday morning my beadle, following the regular Scottish custom, opened the service by carrying the Bible and hymnbook to the pulpit, and returned to open the door to usher me in. At that very moment the girl in question was making her way down the aisle. Without batting an eye he muttered softly to me, "Aye, she's for export only," and it was all I could do to reach the pulpit with a solemn face.

Little did I know that my next move as a minister was almost upon me. It came completely unexpectedly. John Baillie had a charming habit of asking me around to his home occasionally to meet interesting guests from all over the world. One evening, for instance, I sat, entranced, listening to Emil Brunner, the Swiss theologian, whose works were devoured in the Anglo-Saxon Protestant churches because, though they had the same neo-orthodox emphasis as those of Karl Barth, they were easier to understand. (Not too many in Britain or America were able to follow the awesome and resounding argument that broke out between Barth and Brunner. To Brunner's pamphlet on "Natur und Gnade," which I read as a student at Marburg, Barth had replied with one simple piece entitled "Nein!" It is good to think of the ultimate reconciliation of these two great churchmen and to read in the collection of Barth's letters the moving letter he wrote to Brunner on his deathbed.) One night, near the end of 1949, Baillie asked me to come and see him as soon as possible. When I settled into a chair in his study, he gave one of his significant little coughs, which was a sign that he was about to announce something important, and told me the news right away: the University Court had that afternoon agreed to a student request that a chaplain be appointed to the University of Edinburgh, and he wanted me to take the job.

I made the point that I was happy at Greenbank and thought I should stay there a little longer. Then the Baillie batteries leaped into action. There had never been a chaplain at the University before, he told me, because for five hundred years it had been assumed that students were cared for by their local church. I must know as well as he did that this did not apply to the new situation, in which thousands of students came from beyond Scotland and probably only a minority of Scots were active in a church. It was exciting that it was the Students' Representative Council who had pressed for the appointment. My knowledge of the University (I had spent seven years there as a student) would be an asset, he noted, and I had been recently in some demand as a speaker at student conferences. When he had brought up my name, the secretary to the University who had been present at the meeting had intervened to say that it was not his place to offer an opinion, but that he had shared an Oflag (officers' camp) with me in Germany for some eighteen months and agreed with Dr. Baillie's suggestion. So would I say Yes? I staggered away to consult God and my wife—not necessarily in that order. Was this the next step for which God's grace would be given?

I agreed—and a day later the news of the appointment was in the *Scotsman* newspaper. It was hardly the headline of the day, but some were impressed by the students' demand for such an addition to the University staff. I was described as a somewhat maverick minister who combined a passion for German philosophy with a delight in driving an ancient, thoroughly disreputable sports car. My friends wondered why I would want to move out of the mainstream of the parish ministry at this point in my career. I should note that I acquired with the position nothing but a salary and a flat in George Square, the charming eighteenth-century enclave where Sir Walter Scott and other luminaries of Scotland's great literary days had resided. I had no chapel, no office, no secretary, and none of the other conveniences that a resident chaplain would take for granted in the United States.

Once a month, on a Sunday evening, University services were held in the High Kirk of St. Giles', to which prominent preachers from all over the world were invited. It now became my responsibility to conduct these services and to seek out the prominent preachers (who are, as you know, a dying species). I decided right away to begin a regular series of Sunday evening services in the student common-room, hoping to attract not only the faithful but inquirers and agnostics as well. I soon discovered that the faithful preferred to attend one of the churches and that the inquirers had to be sought out. I also arranged to be present in a little room in the Old Quad at certain hours for consultation and counseling. I well remember the first student to show up. He just sat down opposite me and announced, "I don't know who I am." He was not suffering from what is now called an "identity crisis" but was simply referring to a mystery concerning his birth, which we were able to unravel with the help of one of my former parishioners who was a lawyer.

I had to put the chaplaincy on the map. That meant spending a lot of time in the student common-room and anywhere else students frequented. It meant sharing in special occasions like Charities Week and the riotous proceedings connected with the election of a Lord Rector. That year the students chose Sir Alexander Fleming, the inventor of penicillin, and I vividly remember being asked to open the proceedings at the installation. As a former student at Edinburgh, I knew that this occasion would be marked by the wildest outbursts of student exuberance, complete with confetti, rolls of toilet tissue, and occasionally a live hen descending from the galleries. The academic procession was greeted with howls of derision, and the distinguished nominee with boisterous cheers. In the midst of this din, the president of the Students' Representative Council called on me to pray. Although I was seated beside him, I couldn't hear a word he said; I only saw his lips moving. (I then realized why John Baillie—who, as Dean of the Faculty of Divinity, usually gave the invocation on public occasions— had earlier suggested that, since this was a student affair, the chaplain should officiate.) However, I had some confidence in the students, and when I came forward, duly robed, to offer the prayer, there was complete silence for the duration thereof. Later, a visiting French professor expressed his total inability to understand Scots students. "In Paris," he said, "if a distinguished visitor like Sir Alexander Fleming had appeared, he would have been received with dignity and polite applause, but if anyone had dared to offer a prayer, there would have been a riot."

As you can see, this was not exactly a typical framework

in which to operate specifically as a preacher. Even if I elected myself to be the University Preacher at St. Giles' once a year, that, combined with my informal common-room service, didn't offer great scope, though it provided a considerable challenge. I also discovered something negative about my career as a preacher. Being free from duties on Sunday mornings, I accepted invitations to preach in a variety of churches. I learned two things. First, that there is a big difference between preaching to a congregation you know and who knows you, and giving the same sermon to a group of strangers. Second, that this "same sermon" was the problem. Since I was not preaching to basically the same group of people week after week, I was without the stimulation and discipline to conceive and deliver a new sermon each Sunday, and I soon found myself living with one or two favorites. That's why, when I arrived at Madison Avenue years later, I made a private vow to compose an entirely new sermon, completely written out, for every Sunday.

The University years gave me considerable freedom to travel and lecture abroad. In the summer of 1950, Harrison Ray Anderson's earlier invitation materialized in the form of a complete program of preaching and lecturing during the months of July and August. It was to be the first visit to the United States for my wife and me, and I persuaded my banker that the promise of financial rewards for all these engagements entitled me to a huge overdraft with which to pay for our travel. Fortunately, he agreed, and my wife and I departed on a Dutch ship and eventually arrived in Hoboken, New Jersey. I had been allowed to export the sum of fifteen dollars, and I was somewhat shaken to find that this was almost the cost of our taxi fare from Hoboken to Union Seminary, where we had been given a room. On my first Sunday in the United States I preached at Fifth Avenue Church, to which Dr. Bonnell had taken the risk of inviting me. (Perhaps he had consulted with John Baillie. Everybody did.) I was astonished at the size of the congregation on a July morning, and equally astonished at the number of people who expressed appreciation of the sermon after the service. When I returned to Scotland some years ago and was met by the entire congregation after the service,

I found that little had changed in Scottish habits. No one said a word about the sermon except the last parishioner I talked to, who simply said, "When you started, I didn't think it was going to be much. But when you began to argue the point, that was fine!"

That first Sunday I decided that, liturgically, American Presbyterianism was what we used to call "Free Church." It reminded me of the churches like St. George West in Edinburgh, where prayers were mostly extemporaneous, there were no congregational responses, and the sermon came as the climax of the service. The following Sunday I preached at Brick Church and found I had got it all wrong. Thereafter I decided that American churches had forms of worship even more varied than those of Scottish churches, and I reveled in the lively response to the preached Word everywhere. I shall have more to say about the similarities and the differences between church activities in the United States and Britain later, when these ramblings bring me to 1956, the critical year when I began my ministry in New York City.

In 1950 my wife and I were forming our first impressions of the United States. Now, as a fairly seasoned New Yorker, I find it mildly amusing to recollect what these were. Some aspects of the cultural shock come back to me—in no significant order. I remember that my wife and I were overwhelmed by the size and speed of the cars and the noise of the traffic as we sped through the tunnel and wove our way up to Riverside Drive. Everyone seemed in a hurry—which suited me, as I am a naturally impatient person. The automobiles seemed enormous, although we soon discovered that a taxi with soaring fins didn't really hold more people and certainly did not accommodate them more comfortably than a little British cab. The noise in the streets, compounded by that of occasional police cars, fire trucks, and ambulances, seemed to account for the decibel level of ordinary conversation, the rasping shouts for hamburgers and coffee in drugstores, and the shouting that went on even in the luxurious restaurants to which we were occasionally taken. We were puzzled by the almost complete absence of indications as to where the buses and subways were going. (I don't find much improvement now, when a 1986 model bus approaches with little to say about its route but cheerfully advises me to "have a nice day.") When we moved across the country by rail, it was equally strange to find a conspiracy of silence as to the name of any station we passed through.

You may be surprised that, at that time, we were impressed to find New York a surprisingly *clean* city. The streets then were clear of junk, the buildings soared up in glistening splendor, and the citizens all seemed to be wearing spotless white shirts or dresses in spite of the heat and fumes. As a devotee of gadgets, I reveled in all the marvels of American technology, although I found it odd that people preferred to wait in line for an escalator rather than walk up a few steps. We were, of course, impressed by the quantity of goods available in the stores and the ample portions served in the restaurants after the rationing we had become accustomed to in postwar Britain. It was a little alarming to find that a hundred-dollar bill looked exactly the same as a single (not that many hundreds came our way) as we tried to live on five dollars a day.

We soon realized that a New York policeman is not the exact equivalent of a British bobby, whom we regarded as a trim, unarmed, helpful official whom we could turn to when in trouble. Once, in Penn Station, I approached a corpulent cop who appeared to be heavily armed and asked quietly where I might be able to mail a letter (at that time I was having difficulty distinguishing mailboxes from trash cans). I got the answer: "How the hell should I know?" We enjoyed the humor and liveliness of the American version of the English language. There was something Shakespearean about the vigor and vitality of American speech and writing that we found refreshing. When we moved out from under the harness of New York and traveled to the Midwest and the South, we were struck by the warmth and friendliness of nearly all the people we met, the absence of cynicism and complaint among them, and what I can only call the genuine piety of most of them, whether they were church members or not.

In those days there was a delightful arrangement with the railroads whereby ministers could travel at reduced rates. There was even a "Clergy Bureau" staffed for the purpose. Since train travel has always been one of my favorite hobbies (someday, someone should write a thesis analyzing why so many of the clergy are so fond of trains), I was enthralled by the long journeys we took and the peculiar American gadgets to be found in the coaches. (I still adore exploring the mysteries of a roomette.) I was surprised, however, that these palaces on wheels, hauled by gigantic diesels, made such poor time. It was awe-inspiring to watch a freight train pulling over a hundred cars pass a coach. (This was before the lamentable proposal to transport the contents of these cars in the monsters that now clutter up the highways.)

This, then, was the country about which I had heard since childhood—enormous in extent, throbbing with life, inhabited by an incredibly varied population that was, on the whole, tolerant and good-natured. But there were occasional signs that all was not well. We were shocked to see racism for the first time in our lives in a train station down South: it had separate drinking fountains labeled "White" and "Colored." And in Washington, Senator McCarthy was beginning to growl.

Chapter Three

THE POLITICS
OF
THE PASTOR

How, I wondered, did the Church operate in this fascinating country? It didn't take long to discover that, although there was no kind of religious establishment—or perhaps *because* of this situation—churches played a much greater part in national life in the United States than in most European countries. It was the Eisenhower era. Everywhere attendance at worship was extraordinarily high by British standards. It was almost like late Victorian Britain: not to be a churchgoer was somewhat disreputable, if not actually subversive. It seemed as though nothing in the way of a public meeting, lunch, or dinner could happen without an invocation being delivered. Religious books were best-sellers. Billy Graham's crusades were overflowing with huge crowds. New church buildings were springing up in every community as the country fell under the spell of what came to be called "the edifice complex." In sophisticated theological circles, the religious boom was dismissed as superficial, but I felt (not for the last time) that there is a deep-seated religious strain in the American people which is unique in the Western world. It can run to all kinds of extremes and absurdities (as we are witnessing now), but it has deep roots in the nation's history and is a safeguard against the powerful secularist philosophy of academia and the pressures of a culture of abundance.

Preaching in American churches was not all that different from preaching in British churches, except that generally the congregations were more receptive and enthusiastic. This meant, of course, that they were less critical and discriminating. At one conference I attended, I delivered a sermon called "Holy Materialism." I pleaded for an understanding of the Incarnation as having dissolved the rigid distinction between body and soul, and argued consequently that the Gospel must be interpreted in material terms. I was surprised at the enthusiastic response of many hearers, but that evening another preacher delivered an eloquent sermon taking exactly the opposite view of the Gospel, and the same people asked if I didn't think it was splendid. It was then that I began to realize that Americans have not the same taste for theological confrontation as we have in Scotland.

These conferences—or chautauquas, as they were sometimes called—were a new experience for me. I can think of no place in Scotland where people would gather together in large crowds chiefly for the purpose of listening to sermons as many as four or five times a day. True, there were other attractions—entertainments, sports, and excursions—but the people were packed in for the sermons. To my initial discomfiture, I discovered that these sermons were expected to be about fifty minutes long. Since most of mine were the standard twenty minutes in length, I was made to feel on the first few occasions that I had given short measure. (The only other complaint that I sensed was that my accent was not broad enough Scots, which for an Edinburgh man meant that he was not speaking Glasgow.) I decided to consult a seasoned preacher who was a veteran of many such gatherings, and I got the following advice, which I relished but didn't exactly follow: "No problem. Tell 'em three funny stories—and then give 'em hell."

At two conferences in the South I found myself in company with two remarkable men: Toyohiko Kagawa from Japan and, once again, Martin Niemöller. We were billed as three ex-jailbirds who had suffered for their faith. This embarrassed me because in my case it was not true. But the spirit of the publicity had clearly invaded church circles, and I read in the conference newspaper a full spread on the subject, which concluded, "We dare any other chautauqua to beat this line-up." My wife and I thoroughly enjoyed getting to know these two Christian leaders and talking into the night about the role of the Church in the new world. It was also a privilege to get to know American scholars and preachers whose works I had read before and during the war. We didn't always discuss theology. I remember one evening when Reinhold Niebuhr turned on a TV set to introduce us to the drama of all-in wrestling, which he vociferously enjoyed.

My wife and I returned from America that summer with many of our illusions and prejudices shattered and a warm sense of gratitude for the way we had been received and the kindness of our hosts. I hoped another such invitation would come my way, but nothing seemed to whisper that I was being led to throw in my lot with this country which was both such near kin to mine and yet in many ways so foreign. Back home I realized how European I had become. Indeed, at that time I was busy persuading the Church and Nation Committee to convince the General Assembly to pass a motion to urge the government to join the movement for European unity. We did, in fact, put the Church of Scotland behind the proposals that shaped the Common Market years, before either Conservative or Labour governments came reluctantly to the conclusion that Britain should recognize its place in the European community. The Scots have always had a much deeper affinity with our European neighbors than the English, who find it hard to shake off a feeling of ineffable superiority; the Scots have this feeling only toward the English. Therefore, whenever I thought about it at all, I saw my future as involving me in closer ties with the continental churches and in ecumenical student evangelism. And I was still in the thrall of the Scottish preaching tradition.

The American experience had been thrilling. I was particularly impressed by the role of laypeople, who invested so much time, energy, and money in the work of the Church. It became clear to me that what was often scorned in Europe as turning the Church into "big business" was really an expression of serious discipleship that was notoriously lacking in the old countries, where there was still a lingering suspicion of anything like zeal and efficiency in the work of the Church. For the first time it came home to me that it was American Protestantism that had best understood, and put into practice, the biblical doctrine of stewardship—the responsible use of talent, time, and financial resources. I kept in touch with the American scene through reading and by spending time with the many postgraduate American seminarians in Edinburgh. I still had no idea where my main lifework as a minister would lie, although I felt that I should not spend much more time as a university chaplain. On the few occasions when I wondered what God had in store for me, all kinds of possibilities had their attractions, but somehow the pulpit image was difficult to shake off.

The student scene in the early fifties was difficult to assess. It lacked the vigor—not to mention the violence—of the next decade. Politically, the left wing was the most active, and Marxist philosophy was prominent in the debates that went on. The religious arena was quiet. It was unlike my own student days; I met comparatively few flaming atheists or even argumentative agnostics. I did notice that the word "Christian" was being used to describe those who took their religion seriously; it was no longer the blanket label it had been in prewar days, indicating conformity to the traditions of a "Christian" country (as evidenced by the British habit of using the term "Christian name" for "given name" in all documents). The word "Christian" was now being used to refer to students of strong evangelical persuasion, those who would now delight in the redundant expression "born again," but it was also and more frequently used to refer to those who professed belief in Christ as Lord and derived from that belief certain social and political convictions. The Student Christian Movement was active not only in worship and Bible studies but in University politics and the debating societies. In general, however, the student mood was diagnosed as apathetic. There was even, among the numerous clubs and associations, an Apathetic Society—which, of course, never met.

In this atmosphere it was not easy to arouse interest in the Christian Gospel, let alone prompt an enthusiastic response to it. I seldom met with opposition to my activities as chaplain. On the whole, there was a genial tolerance of the presence of a representative of organized religion and an occasional flicker of interest in what he was attempting to do. Once again I saw my task as indicating that I must find a way to express the Christian message in terms that were understandable to a new generation, and that therefore I had to get to know that generation. This meant more thinking about the content of the Gospel as we find it in the Bible, and more study not only of recent theology but of the opposition thinkers. At this time many students and faculty members were heavily influenced by the "logical positivist" philosophy, with its rejection of any beliefs that are not empirically verifiable. Very simply, it means that when I say "I believe in the existence of the Empire State Building" or "I believe in the law of gravity," I am making meaningful statements because they can be verified; but if I say "I believe in God," I am making a meaningless statement—just a noise. The Christian encountering this philosophy is apt to be at a loss, because he or she is not on the old debating ground where believer and unbeliever argued about the truth of their respective positions. For a logical positivist doesn't say "What you believe is untrue," but simply points out that your statement is neither true nor untrue but means nothing at all.

If I had to wrestle with theology (the Bible in one hand), I also had to get to know what was on the minds of those to whom I was supposed to minister (the morning newspaper in the other). So I spent much of my time just mingling with faculty and students, listening and talking. From an American point of view, this was a very unstructured ministry, and I may indeed have wasted a lot of time. Yet I still believe in a relaxed and informal pastoral style rather than a ministry that adheres strictly to timetables, and I am increasingly allergic to the pseudo-scientific jargon of the experts on "pastoral counseling." As should become clear, I firmly believe in the right kind of professionalism for the ministry and resist the current tendency to obliterate the distinction between the clergy and the laity, but God save us from the inhumanity of a mechanized ministry.

University missions were still a feature of student life in

the fifties. (In America they usually called their campaigns something like "Religious Emphasis Week.") If these efforts have largely died out in recent years, the reasons probably lie in the sad fact that most such campaigns found the speakers imported for the occasion talking to the already convinced, appealing for decisions that had already been made, while the unconvinced stayed away in droves. There had been, however, several such missions in the immediate postwar period which aroused a response, notably at Oxford and Cambridge. So I began to accept invitations to lead such missions in various places, the first being two weeks in St. Andrew's. At first we seemed to be making no impact. Services in the beautiful fifteenth-century chapel of St. Salvator were well attended, and a trickle of students found their way to a room designated for private conferences, but on the whole it was the Christian student groups who were the core of the meetings I addressed. But suddenly, toward the end of the mission, the Spirit seemed to move, and at one very well-attended informal meeting where I simply sat with my colleagues answering questions, the whole venture seemed to come to life, and it was clear that serious decisions were being made. It is generally believed that the college interlude is a time of agnosticism and falling away from the Church. For many it still is—hence the importance of confronting the student with the claims of the Gospel in such a way as to effect, if not definite conversions, at least the realization that here is something worth rethinking—and that often bears fruit later, when the serious responsibilities of life come crowding in.

The most exciting mission I have ever shared in was in Australia. In 1952 I accepted an invitation from the Student Christian Movement to lead a two-week campaign in Adelaide and then speak at the Universities of Melbourne, Sydney, Armidale, Brisbane, Canberra, and Perth. Since our summer term was their winter term, I was able to go. After a fascinating flight—the plane stopped in Rome, Beirut, Jakarta, Karachi, Calcutta, and Perth—I was welcomed by the students of Adelaide. The next day I sat with them in the refectory, having been shown an enormous hall, holding over a thousand, where I was due to speak after lunch. Because of my previous experiences, I wondered bleakly what it would be like to speak to a handful of Christian students and the few others they had managed to corral. Suddenly over the loudspeaker came the strident voice of a young man announcing that he was speaking on behalf of the Immaterialist Society. Everyone fell quiet, and the president of the Student Christian Movement explained to me that a member of the opposition had commandeered the microphone. The voice boomed out to the effect that the Immaterialist Society had prepared for this event with a seven-day orgy, and that they were about to conduct an anti-mission meeting to which all were invited. By this time the refectory was alive with shouts and cheers, and my friend had difficulty in reaching the microphone. However, he succeeded in grabbing the mike and announced that the opening address of the mission would start in ten minutes. To my surprise, the entire student body rose and made for the great hall.

Knowing nothing of the situation in Adelaide, I had prepared a series of talks, leaving plenty of room for improvisation. However, I had given my first address the somewhat provocative title of "The End of Agnosticism." When I reached the platform, I saw that the hall was completely filled and that the front rows were occupied by my agnostic opponents—all wearing black armbands. After an elaborate introduction by the president of the university, I arose in a kind of ominous silence. However, my opening words—"Mr. President, friends, and fellow mourners"—evoked a roar of laughter, and I was off. After the meeting we invited everyone to a question-and-answer session in a neighboring classroom. The room was packed, and the session lasted until four o'clock in the afternoon. It was the best frank exchange of views on religion that I have ever taken part in—so good, in fact, that the the following afternoon I offered the floor to the president of the agnostic group, and we had another ding-dong theological battle. From then on the mission was the main event on the campus.

It was an exhausting two weeks, but they were well worth the travel and the fatigue. On recent visits to Australia (some thirty years later), I have met men and women in various walks of life who sought me out to tell me about the influence of that mission. It goes to show what the presence of live opposition can do for the proclamation of the Gospel. I cannot claim the spectacular conversion of the opposition leaders, but before I left they appeared, dressed as wizards, and presented me with a book on logical positivism, inscribed with a quotation from Dr. Johnson: "Much may be made of a Scotchman if he be caught young." The rest of my time in Australia was less tumultuous, but I enjoyed the frankness and openness of the young people in that fascinating country. Before I left, another pulpit-evading temptation came my way—to head a college in Melbourne. It cost me some pangs, and a long-distance telephone call, to decline it.

Another university mission took me to Queen's University at Kingston, Ontario, in midwinter, where I spent a hectic week. I traveled via New York and had the excitement of ringing in the New Year in Times Square with about a million New Yorkers, not one of whom I knew. (I then realized how anyone could be lonely in a teeming city. I missed the joining of hands and the singing of "Auld Lang Syne," as is the Scottish custom. I was, it seemed, with a million noisy individualists, whether rugged or not.) The Christian undergraduate leader at Queen's was a very brilliant student named Don Mathers, who subsequently was a leading spirit in developing the increasingly well-known "Kerygma" Bible-study course. It was a grueling week, not as exacting as my stint at Adelaide, but intellectually demanding. This time I had to put in some time on radio and TV, as well as be interviewed by tough student journalists.

The question naturally began to form in my mind, Why not have a mission at Edinburgh University? The next question was who should lead it. Remembering Jesus' remark that "a prophet is not without honor, save in his own country, and in his own house," I eliminated any idea of my being the main speaker, and set about organizing a campaign to saturate the University with the Christian message, using one outstanding speaker and a team of competent assistants. Besides speakers, I envisaged plays, movies, art exhibitions, and every other possible event that would deliver the message. (Included in these was having someone stand on a table in the student common-room and interrupt the chatter with a brief talk. I remember vividly how, having asked others to do this, I felt compelled to do it myself. It's much easier to preach in Madison Square Garden.) All this required at least a year of preparation. Soon we formed a committee consisting of both staff and students, one that represented as wide a range of theological and denominational points of view as possible. The Anglican chaplain, Pat Rogers, was my right-hand man and an invaluable support. (I like to think that this experience led to his subsequent distinguished career with the World Council of Churches and his later appointment as Bishop of Oxford.) But still the question loomed: Who would be the main speaker?

We decided to ask a Methodist from Sri Lanka called Daniel T. Niles, familiarly known as D. T. He had been busy with evangelism on behalf of the World Council of Churches and was a veteran of many university campaigns. It was, of course, John Baillie who suggested that he was the man for us, and I was delighted when he consented to come. (With his arrival, we made history: it was the first time a native Asian had come to evangelize a Scottish university.) Besides him, we invited about twenty speakers from every field of academic studies and many different Christian communions. They ranged from an expert economist to a Franciscan friar. Niles had the big advantage of firsthand knowledge of Eastern religions. As everyone who talks about religion to Anglo-Saxon students knows, the first question nearly always has to do with other religions. D. T. had his own way of dealing with this question. When a student would ask if the Moslem religion wasn't just as good as the Christian, he would reply, "Are you a Moslem?" If the answer was No, D. T. would say, "The first thing you have to do is to take a look at the religion of your own background. Make up your mind about Jesus Christ. If you decide to reject him, then start investigating Islam and Buddhism." On one occasion when D. T. asked this question, the student replied that he was indeed a Moslem. D. T. answered, "Then you and I have a lot to talk about that others here wouldn't understand. Come around and see me." The student did visit D. T. in our home that evening, and the discussion went on for hours. D. T. never failed to issue this challenge. When I took him to meet the principal of the University, a very distinguished scientist who had helped me by allowing the mission to take place, he asked D. T. about the likelihood that Jesus Christ, who had lived at a certain point in time and space, was the unique Savior of this mysterious universe. D. T. quietly said, "First you have to read the New Testament and make up your mind about him."

It would be nice to say that the mission captured the University for Christ, or even that it led to a sensational revival of religion. It did neither. But the services, the lectures, and the discussions, along with all the other presentations of the Gospel, did make an impact. They proved to me at least that the biblical story of salvation in Christ can be presented in an academic setting without attempting to whittle down the contents and challenge of the historic Christian faith or encouraging the growth of little cells of spirituality that fear to face the major questions of the hour.

Not long after this I found myself once again interrupting the chatter of the student common-room. It was a dramatically sad occasion. A messenger from the principal had slipped in and whispered to me the news that had just been announced—the death of King George the Sixth. The students were stunned when I communicated the news, and in the silence that followed I offered a prayer. There are some men and women in high office who seem to attract a special kind of devotion in people who may never have seen them. King George was one of them. No one ever forgot how he and his Queen remained in London throughout the blitz; they knew firsthand the horrors of bombing.

About this time there was a similar kind of grieving in Edinburgh. Sir John Fraser, a former principal of the University and a brilliant and dedicated surgeon whose clients had ranged from the highest in the land to the poorest of the Edinburgh slums, died unexpectedly. Since he was the man who had saved my life in 1924 when I was succumbing to a critical attack of peritonitis, I naturally went to his funeral at St. Giles'. But I couldn't get in. The square outside the church was packed with people like me who wanted to pay their respects to this great man. Afterwards a student told me of meeting an old woman from the Canongate (the poorest part of the city) with tears streaming down her face. All she could say was, "Ma doctor's deid."

When King George died, some memories naturally surfaced. During my first visit to Balmoral he had been away in London because of the war crisis, but the Queen told me that she had phoned him and relayed my sermon to him. When I was working our illegal radio in the prison camp, one of my most thrilling moments was hearing the King's voice on D day and the ending of his speech: "The Lord will give strength unto his people; the Lord will bless his people with peace." I remembered my second visit to Balmoral after the war, and the impression I had gotten that the King was a sincere Christian who could speak his mind forcibly when the necessity arose, but who also had a lively sense of fun. One remark of his at dinner had a significance that I didn't understand at the time.

"Are you one of my chaplains?" he demanded.

I replied that I had been a chaplain during the war.

"I don't mean that," he said. "Are you one of my domestic chaplains here in Scotland?"

"No, sir," I said. "That position is usually held by senior men like former Moderators."

"That's what I had in mind," he answered. "I want some younger ones."

Thus it was that soon after Queen Elizabeth's accession I received the appointment to be one of Her Majesty's chaplains in Scotland. It was a position I naturally valued as a minister of the Church of Scotland. The news was received with some astonishment, because I was by far the youngest ever to be appointed. I believe I am also the only chaplain to have resigned owing to my later departure for New York.

And how did that come about? In 1953—at the invitation of Pitney Van Dusen, a president of Union Theological Seminary, and Dr. John Sutherland Bonnell of Fifth Avenue Presbyterian Church—I returned to the United States to give another round of lectures and sermons. My wife was with me, and we enjoyed our second trip immensely. After Scotland, we even liked the heat. Once again the topic of evangelism was in the air. At Union I gave lectures based on my book *The Commu-*

nication of the Gospel and had the pleasure of meeting that master of homiletics, Halford Luccock, who had just published a book with exactly the same title. I was also in the care of Jesse Bader, who headed the Evangelism Committee of the National Council of Churches and was a member of the Christian Church, known as Disciples. His charm and enthusiasm for the cause were infectious, and it was an honor for me to be invited to Melbourne some years ago to give lectures on evangelism ("Go—and Make Disciples") in memory of this great man.

Politically it was not an easy time in the United States. On my first visit in 1950, the Korean War had just broken out, and in 1953 the armistice negotiations were still dragging on. On our arrival this time, my wife and I were a little surprised at the questions we were asked about our possible Communist affiliations and any lurking desires to overthrow the U.S. government by force. I got my first taste of the McCarthy era when I was asked what I thought about the accusation that U.S. churches were in the front line of Communist propaganda. I risked immediate deportation by laughing at the very idea. However, I soon understood the blanket of suspicion that hung over the country. I realize now that there was such a thing as espionage, and that Communism is not exactly a joke; still, I am convinced that the way to meet its threat is not by imitating its methods and morals. Of course, at that time it was difficult to adjust to the fact that while in Britain we had been tearing down air-raid shelters for some time, here in America they were building new ones.

Once again I enjoyed preaching and the response I received in America. On the way home I kept feeling that the next step was drawing near, and soon after returning I was immersed in a cloud of rumor about my future. Dr. Warr of St. Giles' was retiring, and there was much talk about his successor. Mine was not, of course, the only name being suggested, but it was difficult to brush off the idea that I might be chosen—especially when one journalist, hot on the trail, went so far as to phone me with the "news" that I had been selected and ask for a comment. Mine was brief, to the effect that he knew more than I did. For me it was a dilemma. Every ancestral instinct responded to the thought of holding the pulpit of John Knox, and this was not the kind of offer to be refused. On the other hand, I had no desire to spend the rest of my life in Edinburgh—and neither, very definitely, did my wife. We had both been born and raised in the area; I had spent my school days there, followed by four years at the University and then three at New College, and later had had a parish there. I mean no disrespect to a city I love when I say that we had had enough of Edinburgh. In addition, St. Giles' is, to put it crudely, a lousy place to preach. The acoustics of the church then demanded that one address one's remarks to the pillar opposite the pulpit, and I knew how often these remarks had to take into account the presence of dignitaries of all kinds having their annual "kirking." These were cramping conditions under which to expound the Scriptures and proclaim the Gospel.

Troubled, I went to see John Baillie. His first wise remark was that it was quite probable that I would not go to St. Giles'. When he was proved right by the appointment of another "front-runner" to the post, I went to see him again and asked where he thought I should go, since I wanted to leave the University chaplaincy. His first question was, "Do you want to preach or to teach?"—and he had me stumped. Lurking in the back of my mind was the knowledge that the chair that had been occupied by his brother, Donald Baillie (whose book *God Was in Christ* had won a worldwide reputation), was now vacant, owing to his tragic death, but I didn't have the nerve to raise the subject. "Go thou and preach. . . ." Was I pushing the pulpit away? We discussed various possibilities in Scotland. Then John asked me if I had ever thought of going to America. I confessed that I had enjoyed my visits there but didn't want to settle in that country. Finally, to my astonishment, he said, "Why don't you apply for Donald's chair at St. Andrew's?"

I managed to stammer, "Do you think I could catch up with the theology?" I knew that he was aware of how little serious theological work I had been doing recently.

"Yes," he said. Then came the little cough. *"If you work."*

Then came the third American tour for my wife and me.

It was the summer of 1955. My first engagement was to spend July preaching at Deer Park Church in Toronto, where the congregations were large and enthusiastic. Being in Toronto also meant contact with a few of the thirty-odd first cousins of mine living in that city. During this period, I had a date to speak at Princeton Seminary, and I will never forget my journey there. Since I was due to leave on a certain night but first had to conduct an evening service at Deer Park, I wondered how I would get to the airport in time to catch my plane. To my surprise, my host telephoned the police, and I was provided with an escort to the airport. It was hair-raising, not only to be in a car running all the lights in downtown Toronto but to be escorted by a state trooper traveling at ninety miles an hour whom my driver had trouble following. The next day, however, I was safely back in Toronto.

I was to be at one church for the whole of August, but between finishing my July engagement and beginning this one I was to preach at the original Chautauqua in western New York. While there I fell in with a few well-known churchmen, including that great preacher Paul Scherer. One evening the talk ran to church gossip, and I learned that, since George Buttrick had retired, the pulpit of Madison Avenue was vacant. Names of possible successors were bandied about, but it never even occurred to me that I would hear the name of this church again. Eventually I reached New York City, and my wife and I settled in for a sticky August.

Chapter Four

FROM EDINBURGH TO NEW YORK

A good friend had lent my wife and me a tiny apartment on 10th Street just off Fifth Avenue. We enjoyed exploring Greenwich Village, which is like no other village we had ever seen, and discovered the off-Broadway theatres. On the Saturday night before my first appearance at Fifth Avenue Church, we decided to spend precious dollars on two tickets for the Broadway production of *Cat on a Hot Tin Roof*, with Burl Ives in the leading role. We returned, physically and mentally exhausted, some time after midnight, only to discover that we had left our only key inside the apartment. I tried every trick I had learned as a P.O.W., but to no avail, so we went to a hotel just around the corner on Fifth Avenue. It took me about an hour to convince the authorities there to admit a couple with no luggage and without visible means of support, but eventually they accepted our story, and we were assigned a room.

That was all very well, but in that inaccessible apartment reposed not only all our luggage, including my church robes, but the sermon I intended to preach that very morning. So I resolved to make one more attempt to storm the fortress: I telephoned the police and asked them to meet my wife and me at the apartment. In five minutes a car rolled up, and two cops sprang out who looked as if they meant business. Their first act was to ring every bell in the apartment building. One by one doors and windows opened, and anxious faces peered out as the cry "Police!" rang out. In ten minutes it was made clear that no one had any idea how to get into our apartment, and the police departed, kindly wishing us well. Then my wife had a bright idea. She had the telephone number of the chauffeur of the lady who had lent us the apartment. We awoke him from his slumbers, and about two hours later he arrived and let us in. I had about two hours' sleep before setting out for the church.

I remember thinking what a disaster such a preliminary adventure would have been if I had been making a critical appearance in front of a congregation interested in offering me a call. What I didn't know was that, in a sense, this was exactly what it was. For after the service several of the elders remarked to me, "There were a lot of people from Madison here this morning." Anyway, I got through the service, and if I looked haggard and had a croaky voice, it was probably attributed to the effect of the heat and humidity on a wandering Scot. The next day I set off for Montreat for a round of sermons and lectures, giving only an occasional thought to the significance of the presence of visitors from Madison Avenue at that service.

On this trip I enjoyed the beauties of the North Carolina countryside, climbed a mountain, tried to keep my lamentable golf game a secret, and learned for the first time how to distinguish Southern Presbyterians from Northern. I found a new friend to argue with—Mac Crowe—who at that time was a leading opponent of any attempt to unite the two churches. When he claimed that in the South they had remained true Presbyterians, faithful to the Westminster Confession, I pointed out that, as far as I could judge, they were anything but Presbyterian in the informal style of worship they had borrowed from their Baptist and Methodist neighbors. This worried him a lot, and the next time we met he told me of introducing his flock to the dignities of the historic Reformed liturgies and the metrical psalms. He also acknowledged that Southern prejudices about such things as smoking and drinking were not part of our Presbyterian heritage, while I was willing to confess that both in the northern section of the United States and in Scotland we had suffered from theological laxity during the ultra-liberal period. I did, however, try to pin him down by asking if he would insist on the paragraph in the Westminster Confession that follows the one on "the elect": "The rest of mankind God was pleased, according to the unsearchable counsel of his own will, whereby he extendeth or withholdeth mercy as he pleaseth, for the glory of his sovereign power over his creatures, to pass by, and to ordain them to dishonor and wrath for their sin, to the praise of his glorious justice." Mac was the first American pastor I had met who genuinely loved a theological argument, and we remained good friends over many years until his untimely death in a car accident.

When I returned from Montreat to our little nest on 10th Street, my wife told me that a gentleman who identified himself as an elder in Madison Avenue Presbyterian Church had been telephoning regularly to fix a time to have lunch with me. This is beginning to sound serious, I thought, but a free lunch was not to be despised. The elder turned out to be a charming architect named Harold Sleeper, and over lunch we had a fascinating conversation that ranged over almost every interesting topic except the vacant pulpit at Madison Avenue. Finally, after he had asked for the bill, he shyly announced, "I ought to tell you that I have been deputed by the vacancy committee of Madison Avenue Presbyterian Church to find out if your mind is completely closed to the thought of accepting a call on this side of the Atlantic." I replied that, although I had not felt that I was being led in that direction (St. Andrew's was still the setting in which I saw myself in the future), it would not be true to say that I had firmly decided never to accept a call in America. On this note we went our separate ways.

The next Sunday I was informed by my spies that more members of Madison Avenue were present among the Fifth Avenue congregation than the week before. So in the afternoon my wife and I decided that we would at least walk up Madison Avenue to 73rd Street and have a cautious look at the church. When nobody seemed to be around, we slipped into the sanctuary and moved very quietly up a side aisle. At that point a voice rang out from the chancel: "If you two's reckoning on getting married, it's the center aisle you use!" It was a helpful little janitor who was giving us this advice.

"Thanks for the compliment," I said, "but we're just having a look." We liked what we saw. This was not an auditorium dominated by the pulpit but a place to worship. Already I could think of certain improvements, but they had to wait until the grace that had led me "thus far" began to operate in strange ways. At this point the thought of a New York pastorate had not yet taken the shape of a live option.

The next week I was forced to meet this decision head-on. My wife and I were invited to meet those of the vacancy committee who were in New York, as well as the other ministers of the church. The chairman of the committee was Ogden Purves, a wonderful man to whom I and (more importantly) my wife were immediately drawn. He drew a picture of the kind of church they represented: one with a tradition of strong preaching but also with a church house where all kinds of things happened. He spoke of the history of serving the needs of a very diverse community, of the cosmopolitan nature of the congregation, and of the challenge of a ministry in an exciting city, an international nexus with strong currents of thought, both religious and secular. As others joined in the talk, it was obvious to me that this was not a single-class, conventional, comfortable congregation that was looking for a preacher to give them little more than a spiritual kick once a week. As they contemplated the future of their church, they meant business—in the New Testament sense of the word. The clergy present—Frank Grebe, Montague White, and Victor Baer—all of whom were to become and remain dear friends of mine, had with George Buttrick formed a collegium in which each one had equal authority and status. I thought that arrangement somewhat unusual but assumed (wrongly) that it was common in the United States. Anyway, status has never seemed to me to be an important ingredient in the call to the ministry, and I liked what I saw of the men with whom the new preacher would have to work.

The call then gradually took shape, and it was clear that a decision would be made within a week or so. The following Sunday I arrived at Fifth Avenue Church. They have a charming custom of bringing a group of elders into the robing room before the service to welcome the preacher of the day; one of them usually issues an invitation to lunch. A prayer is offered, and then the preacher proceeds to the pulpit. Fifth Avenue has always been, and still is, one of the best-attended churches in New York City, and it was very impressive, on a hot and sticky August day, to be confronted with well over a thousand worshipers gently waving the little fans that were provided.

My text that morning came from the story of Elijah in the nineteenth chapter of the First Book of Kings. The prophet had emerged the victor in his classic contest with the prophets of Baal, and now the fierce Queen Jezebel had sworn revenge, and her court had become too dangerous for him. "He arose, and went for his life." A few days later, in a suicidal mood, he took refuge in a cave. And that's where I got my text: "And he came thither unto a cave, and lodged there; and, behold, the word of the Lord came to him, and he said unto him: 'What doest thou here, Elijah?' " I explored that cave thoroughly. It was the hiding place of a man who was scared to continue to face the complexities of Jezebel's court and the risks of an active role in the controversies of the day. It was the symbol of our longing for a religion that offers quiet and comfort rather than challenge. Psychologically it represented the desire that lurks in us all to return to the peace and satisfactions of the womb.

Then something happened that is part of the risk of this preaching business. Even as I was directing this flow of pulpit rhetoric (I use the word in its good old meaning, not its new bad one), a voice within me was saying, "Yes, David, the cave—that's St. Andrew's for you." And after the service, the first thing my wife said to me was, "You were preaching to yourself this morning." I hasten to add that I knew that the voice was meant for me alone that morning. It didn't come as a blanket indictment of anyone who chose to be a seminary professor rather than a preacher. It was for me that this grace was given at this particular time in my career, that I heard again the call to preach. I was forty-five. It was time to take a risk, to respond to a call to a parish that was to me unknown, in a city which had once been described to me as "the graveyard of preachers." Still, I wanted to talk it over with somebody from the old country. But with whom, and how?

Grace once again offered the answer. As I ascended the

pulpit steps for the afternoon service that day, who should be sitting in a front pew but James S. Stewart, the preacher who had meant so much to me when I was a student and young minister and who now *was* a seminary professor. We had a long talk in the robing room after the service. It was now becoming clearer and clearer to me what my answer was going to be. But I needed one more voice to confirm my instincts. So, of course, I sent off a cable to John Baillie. He told me later that, since he was in Switzerland when he received it, it cost him nearly all his foreign exchange to send me an adequate reply. It was nicely balanced, clearly reasoned—and encouraging. I told dear Ogden Purves that he would have a Yes or a No the next day.

But the grace of God often comes through less obvious channels than saints and scholars. This time it came to me in a quite ridiculous guise. That Sunday night we were dining with an American friend at the Westbury on Madison at 69th Street. For me it was rather a restless meal. Between courses I would excuse myself to go out and pace the avenue. I was looking north to where I believed Madison Avenue was situated a few blocks away. On my last exit I saw something I hadn't noticed before. High up above the buildings a bright light was shining. "Come on!" it seemed to be saying to me. "Come on! Come on!" When I returned to my coffee, I knew that the decision was made. It was only later that I discovered that my celestial light was the beacon on the top of the Carlyle Hotel.

The next morning my wife and I were awakened at an early hour by a ring of our doorbell. I thought it could only be a telegram, perhaps from John Baillie. My wife was more anxious about the state of our little apartment, which was not arranged for visitors. In my pajamas I opened the door. There stood Ogden Purves. And there in the chaos I delivered my Yes to the call.

There was, of course, a lot to talk about—exactly when I should assume the position, where my wife and I would live (George Buttrick's apartment on 79th Street was too big for us), and when and how the news should be released. I didn't want the principal of Edinburgh University to learn of my impending departure from a press release, nor—worse—the Queen to find out from the London *Times* that one of her chaplains was proposing to leave the country. Naturally I wrote my father and mother and told them the news in confidence. Then I sent a picture postcard to my friend Pat Rodgers, the Anglican chaplain. To preserve secrecy I wrote it in Greek. He was puzzled, he told me later, at the content of my message until he realized that it was written in English with Greek characters. Anyway, he got the point and remained silent.

After I had finished my duties with our good friends at Fifth Avenue, my wife and I set out on our return voyage to Edinburgh in September. In what was to become our regular custom, I went by ship and she went by plane. This procedure had nothing to do with any theory that the world could not afford the simultaneous loss of two such important people in a plane crash. It simply resulted from the fact that I revel in ships, from freighters to the *QEII*, whereas my wife begins to feel seasick the moment she crosses the gangway. So we said good-bye to Ogden Purves, and to our little apartment (whose key we were now very careful to take with us). My wife came to the dock to see me off, and soon I was leaning over the rails watching the outline of our new home glide by as the ship slipped down the Hudson. It was when we were passing the end of the island and I looked over to 10th Street that I suddenly felt something unexpected in my pocket. It was the key to the apartment, which I had forgotten to give my wife. Since I was informed by the ship's authorities that it could not be handed to the pilot for delivery, I will leave the rest of that story to your imagination.

Since we had agreed that the transition would take place at the beginning of 1956, the three intervening months were a flurry of activity interspersed with reflections on the change we were making. Early on there came a telegram bearing the name (charming, I thought) of Kennebunkport. It was from Ogden and bore the news that the congregation of Madison Avenue Presbyterian Church had unanimously approved the call. It was a comfort to know that in this enterprising new country to which I was headed, Presbyterians still did things "decently and in order." While in Edinburgh we had to make arrangements for travel, for visas (getting these from the consulate in Glasgow gave me my first experience of American bureaucracy at its worst), for the transportation of our household goods, and for a place to stay while the apartment that had been secured on 90th Street was being furnished. (We were the guests of Campbell and Barbara Burton during that interim, a period which I had reckoned would be about three weeks but which turned out to be three months. We didn't know that in New York you couldn't go to a store, as we did in Edinburgh, point to a chair, and say "I'll have that," and find it delivered the next day. But the Burtons were wonderful hosts during our extended stay, and initiated us tactfully into the mysteries of American life.) There was little time for any second thoughts about the decision I had made—nor had I any. But I was, of course, curious about the nature of American church life, since I was about to become a part of it, not just a peripatetic preacher sampling it. I decided—rightly, it turned out—that the central things would be similar to what I had known in Coldstream and Greenbank: conducting services, preaching, and pastoral work were not going to be very different. But the administration, the management, the whole machinery of church life—these, I knew, were going to be a new experience. And they were.

The preaching assignment that loomed ahead of me had to be thought through. By this time I knew enough of the American scene to realize that preachers there still had a kind of prominence that was fast disappearing in Britain. At that time, what you might call "well-known" preachers—a class now almost extinct—were thick on the ground. I knew I should have to battle the temptation to play to the crowds. Therefore—to return to Karl Barth's image—I would have to strengthen the hand that held the Bible, and not let the hand holding the morning newspaper dominate my thinking. I also decided that I would do everything I could to counter the tendency to think of worship as an assortment of hymns, prayers, doxologies, and glorias leading up to the great moment of the sermon. During these months of reflection, I was aware that I was finally responding to "this grace given." Provided other things worked out well, the post at Madison Avenue was likely to be my major lifework—and preaching was going to be a big part of it. I heard the text from which my title comes: "Unto me, who am less than the least of all saints, is this grace given, that I should preach among the Gentiles the unsearchable riches of Christ." In the Bible I had carried through the war, this verse was distinctly marked. That was me—"less than the least of all saints." That was the call and the equipment—"this grace given." That was the theme—"the unsearchable riches of Christ." The only word that didn't quite fit was "Gentiles." After arriving in the United States, I wondered facetiously why, if God had wanted me to preach to the Gentiles, he should have sent me to New York. But in a more serious vein, I have interpreted Paul's Gentiles as those of our contemporaries who have lost nearly all contact with the Church—and there are plenty of them in New York. So obviously evangelism was to be an important note in my preaching in the years ahead.

In the light of my experience as a wandering preacher, I made two private vows. The first was that every sermon I prepared for the morning service at Madison Avenue would be, to the utmost of my ability, a new one. Never would I dish up an amended version of some favorite sermon from the barrel. I knew I would inevitably repeat certain themes, and that illustrative stories might reappear over the years. But I was determined that each sermon would be conceived afresh under the guidance of the Spirit, and I was convinced that the contents of the Bible would reveal more and more of "the unsearchable riches of Christ." As an itinerant preacher, I would naturally repeat sermons I had already given, but for my own flock it was imperative that I preach a new sermon every Sunday. I felt all the more strongly the need to explore afresh these "unsearchable riches," since to me it has always been an awesome and sometimes disturbing thought that regular churchgoers who listen for years to the same preacher may be overinfluenced in their understanding of the Christian faith by his favorite themes and hobbyhorses. This vow I have kept for thirty years, and I mean to keep it in such years as may be ahead.

The other vow flowed from the first. I determined that I would write down every word of each of these new sermons.

This vow I have kept with only one exception—the time that I came back from a visit to Berlin on a Saturday night and then spoke extempore the next morning on "Walls." This doesn't mean that I believe in reading sermons. Each must communicate directly with a congregation. And any sensitive and sensible preacher knows that there are times to diverge from the script or to add what the Spirit prompts. But in order to counter intellectual laziness, to be sure the work is done to the best of one's ability, and to feel free to worship with a congregation without making a frantic mental review of the points of a sermon during hymns and prayers, the discipline of writing is, for me at least, essential. The other aspect of the sermon—the sensitivity to the real needs of the listeners—was, I realized, going to be more of a difficulty. I knew it would take time to become familiar with the New York scene, with the enormously varied types of people attending my new church— even to learn the language. When I began my American ministry, I still had the naive idea that there were only about a dozen words that had different meanings on the two sides of the Atlantic. As I soon discovered, there are hundreds if not thousands of words and expressions of this kind. I remember my first secretary, a gentle and devout young lady of Methodist background, bursting into my study waving the latest page of a sermon I had given her and insisting, "Dr. Read, you surely didn't mean to say that!" It's just as well I can't remember now what the gaffe was, for I'm sure it was unprintable.

Besides the language problem, there was the prospect of getting to know another culture, understanding other traditions, adjusting to new loyalties, learning about the different backgrounds from which people come, and being sensitive to a new set of fears and joys, ideals and prejudices. My previous visits and some reading in American history helped in this regard, but I knew that there was still much I had to learn. As someone once pointed out, a Britisher should not assume that a common language means that Americans will have similar roots and points of view, and then be annoyed by startling differences. It is much better to start off with the assumption that the United States is a foreign country, and then be delighted with the similarities one finds. Among these similarities are certain basics for an imported preacher. There is no original American or British sin; we meet on common ground. And there is no distinctive grace of God with an American or a British label. Since the Gospel deals with human beings as such, and since our deepest needs are for the forgiveness of our sins and the empowering that comes with the grace of God, a preacher should really be at home anywhere on earth.

On New Year's Eve I boarded the Cunard liner *Ivernia* at Liverpool, and we slipped comfortably over to Ireland before heading for the wintry Atlantic. As I sat in the lounge watching a steward putting up decorations for the festivities of what the Scots call "Hogmanay," I thought how marvelous it was going to be to celebrate my new move in 1956, and how I wished my wife could be with me for the occasion—perhaps risking seasickness for once. An hour later, however, I didn't like the look of the party preparations, and didn't feel at all inclined to have another drink. Shortly thereafter, I retired to my berth, from which I didn't emerge until we docked at Halifax a week later. I began to think fondly of airplane travel. In short, it was a hideous journey, and I was glad when the *Ivernia* finally came within sight of New York, and we came forging up the ice-covered Hudson to dock in the old Cunard berth.

As I descended the gangway in my black coat and Anthony Eden homburg, I noticed a row of four cheerful men lined up in greeting, and soon I felt the embrace of my new colleagues. I was thus completing what came to be known as Madison Avenue's monosyllabic ministry: White, Grebe, Baer, and Read, supported by minister emeritus Hood and organist and choirmaster Lee. After being whisked up to the church and over to the Burtons to deposit my bags, I entrained for Boston and a memorable weekend. I say "memorable," but, unfortunately, my memory is not sufficient to record all that was said during a weekend with my predecessor, George Buttrick.

We talked most of that weekend, and I began to learn more and more about the congregation he spoke of with deep affection. On Sunday morning, as I was having breakfast with Mrs. Buttrick, I heard strange sounds coming from the study next door. "Don't worry," she said. "That's just George going over his sermon." I felt at home because I used to like to do just that, although now I find I can hear myself preaching without actually letting it boom out. It was a great experience to hear that sermon later in the Memorial Church at Harvard, which was packed with students, but there was also something daunting about hearing my predecessor at the top of his form. I remembered that *his* predecessor had been Henry Sloane Coffin, and I wondered, not for the first time, why God had been pushing me into their pulpit. But I needn't have worried that George would shadow me. One thing that he had repeated that weekend was, to use his own words, "I'll not get in your hair." He was true to that promise—indeed, so much so that for the next five years I had the greatest difficulty in persuading him to return to Madison Avenue. Eventually he agreed to a very welcome annual visit, and we had the pleasure of celebrating the fiftieth anniversary of his ordination in his old church.

The press seemed to me to be strangely interested in my arrival and in my first sermon. It is odd now to remember that in the fifties both the *New York Times* and the *Herald Tribune* devoted a whole page of their Monday-morning editions to the reporting of sermons. When I once complained to that wise old Scot, Jim McCracken, who had succeeded Harry Emerson Fosdick at Riverside, that the sermon reports seemed somewhat tame and often ill-chosen, he replied, "David, we get kid-glove treatment. What about the reviews of plays and movies? How would you like to read that 'Read yesterday fell well below his predecessor's standard and even his own. His voice sounded tired, and his delivery was wretched. Et cetera, et cetera'?" One of the first signs I had that the religious boom of the fifties had run its course was the elimination of sermon reports in the press a few years later. For almost twenty-five years thereafter, you would never see a report of a sermon in a New York City paper—unless a furious controversy was raging, or the preacher had just got himself arrested. I'm not complaining. Journalists, I believe, have pretty shrewd ideas about what really interests the public.

From the beginning I felt at ease with my colleagues and at home with the large and varied congregation. As the months passed, it became clearer and clearer to me that, despite my wrigglings, the call to preach was being fulfilled. Sermon preparation is not always a delight. It means hard work, the discipline of getting down to it, whether or not one feels in the mood. I was helped in this by a pressure unknown to me in Scotland—the demands of a printed bulletin, which meant a decision on topic, text, and Scripture readings by Tuesday noon. Giving a title to a sermon was also a requirement to which I was unaccustomed. At times I resented it; then I found that it did help me to concentrate on what the sermon was really about. It was also a challenge to find a title that was neither too clever nor insufferably dull. What I did experience was that inexpressible moment that everyone who is called to and trained for a particular job occasionally experiences. I mean that sense of joy and satisfaction that sometimes comes (for me it happens during the actual delivery of a sermon) when you think to yourself, "Yes, this is what I am meant to be doing." As a precaution against the temptation to think of preaching simply as an art to which I was dedicated, I used to remind myself of the first pulpit in which I preached as a young seminarian. A brass plate was affixed on it so that it could be seen only by the preacher; it read, "Sir, we would see Jesus." I have also tried to keep in mind the words applied in the prologue of John's Gospel to the preaching of John the Baptist: "He was not that Light, but was sent to bear witness of that Light."

At first I made few changes in the liturgy except for introducing—or perhaps I should say "reintroducing"—the practice of having nearly all baptisms celebrated before the congregation at public worship, and suggesting the use of the first order of Holy Communion in the Book of Common Worship, which was the one I was used to in Scotland. I was becoming more and more convinced that the power and efficacy of these two sacraments had been sadly neglected in recent Presbyterian practice, and that we needed to recover the Reformed tradition which bound Word and sacrament together in the worship of God and the response to the Gospel. Later we were to adopt the original Reformed liturgy, in which the sermon comes in the middle of the service as an exposition of the written Word, and is followed by prayers and the offering and, as often as possible, by baptism or the Lord's Supper. I don't like tinkering with an order of worship. (I remember C. S. Lewis's tongue-in-cheek remark to the effect that "I don't care what order the rector uses, provided he doesn't change it!") What seems important to me is that a congregation should know the meaning of each act in the drama of worship and the significance of any changes. In general, it could be said that nearly all the changes we have made at Madison Avenue have been designed to increase the participation of the whole congregation. It is ironic that the changes effected by the Reformation—which strove to bring back such participation at a time when congregations tended to be mere spectators of what was going on in the chancel—should have lapsed, in only a few centuries, into a form of worship in which the congregation became passive auditors, with the minister doing nearly everything, including all the praying. It was certainly not the intention of Luther and Calvin to replace passive spectators with passive listeners.

There was one quite literal shock in store for this transplanted Scot. You must have noticed that the information you acquire about another country before you visit it is very unsatisfactory. Nobody tells you about features that strike you almost as soon as you arrive. One thing nobody had told me about was the phenomenon of static electricity, which is unknown in Britain. Just before I arrived at Madison Avenue, a very generous member had provided thick carpeting for the entire sanctuary, including two center aisles down which the ushers proceeded with the offering. You can guess what happened the first time I received a silver plate. It was like a sign from heaven, though that wasn't the word I nearly said.

These early years meant trying to get to know as many as possible in this assorted congregation. There were a lot of Scots, who spoke the same language as I did, but there were also people who talked to me in French or German. There seemed to be people from all over the world, including many Chinese. Thinking of the regular pastoral visitation that was common in Scotland, I proposed to my colleagues that we begin to call on each household, announcing every Sunday that the ministers would be calling that week on members who lived in a particular area—73rd Street or whatever. My colleagues gave me a skeptical look but sportingly agreed to the plan. After about a month of making futile telephone calls, struggling to find names and numbers in dark hallways, ringing bells that didn't produce an answer, and finding fewer and fewer evenings free for such expeditions, I came to see that what was practicable in suburban Edinburgh wouldn't work in New York. To my regret, I've had to settle for what you might call "crisis visits."

There was another new factor for me in my life as a preacher: the demand of outside engagements—requests that I travel to different parts of the country to preach or lecture. It took me a while to realize that going to Chicago from New York was not like going to Glasgow from Edinburgh, and that traveling from New York to Texas took even longer than traveling from Edinburgh to London. When I realized that to accept most of these invitations would make inroads on my timetable, I went to consult an elder who, I knew, was a wise, dedicated, and very straightforward person. He listened as I explained my quandary and then told me that it was good for Madison Avenue's preacher to become known beyond New York, and that some of these engagements were important. Then he leaned forward and tapped the table. "But remember," he said, "Madison Avenue comes first." I sometimes hear that voice now, years after his death, and am grateful for it.

We are not yet out of the fifties in this meandering story. (I sometimes wonder, Does God's grace meander? We always want it to be available, "on tap.") The convulsions of the sixties lay ahead. My excuse for spending so much time on this period of my life is that over the years I have been asked one question more often than any other—"How did you happen to come to America?"—with its corollary: "Why did you leave Scotland to come to New York?" I hope I have supplied some of the answers. What follows will indicate why, with each passing year, I have become more certain that this decision was ultimately dictated not by a passing whim or the toss of a coin but by a grace that was given. There is *some* truth, you know, behind that awesome word "predestination."

Chapter Five

THE
TURBULENT
SIXTIES

If I ever had doubts that accepting a call to New York would plunge me into the center of world events, they were soon dispelled. Within months of my arrival, both the Hungarian revolution and the Suez crisis erupted. They were symbolized for me one October evening in 1956 as I left the old Biblical Seminary on 49th Street, where I had been giving a lecture. There in front of me was the towering United Nations building, and every light was burning at eleven o'clock at night. I said a prayer for the world's diplomats and walked home, pondering again the perpetual question of how a preacher of the Gospel addresses the social and political issues of the day.

The simplest answer is that they can be left alone. Indeed, there were many features in my homiletical training that urged me to do just that. My task was to expound the Scriptures and present "Jesus Christ, the same yesterday, today, and forever." I had to have confidence that delivering the challenge of the Gospel and building up a congregation in the faith would result in the nurturing of Christian men and women who would respond to the acute questions of the day with decisions based on their religious convictions. Had not Paul, whose activities brought him into lively contact with the affairs of the Roman Empire and its restless subjects, been content with the words he heard from Christ: "My grace is sufficient for thee"? There is little in the Book of the Acts or in the epistles to suggest that the first Christian preachers had much to say about current controversies or indulged in political propaganda. What is recorded about their attitude toward the policies of Rome is somewhat ambiguous. On the one hand, they seemed grateful for the stability of society in the Empire and gladly took advantage of the relatively safe network of communications for the rapid spread of the Gospel. Thus both Paul and Peter are on record as commending obedience to the civil powers except under circumstances in which Christians would be required to deny their Lord. On the other hand, the Book of the Revelation—a comparatively late document—indicates in its own cryptic and luridly metaphorical style that the Church came to a point of denouncing the Empire and viewing the emperor as the Antichrist.

In Scotland there were many church members who resented the intrusion of political judgments into the proclamation of the Word, and were less than happy with the pronouncements of the Church and Nation Committee of the General Assembly. I soon found that many in the United States shared this point of view. "When I go to church on Sunday," many were saying, "I don't want to have my nose rubbed in the controversies I live with all the working week. I want something different, something spiritual." In my first parish I had tried to provide that something different, although the Munich crisis in 1938 had disturbed my complacency. To a congregation who expected me to rejoice with them that Mr. Chamberlain had brought us "peace in our time," I offered the verse that says, "He gave them their request but sent leanness into their soul."

My prison-camp preaching raised this issue in a different way. Any references to world events, and particularly to the devices of the Nazis, had to be clothed in allusive language verging on that of the Book of the Revelation. A nearer parallel would be the issue of relating the sermon to specific moral problems in our camps. I learned a lot from an incident that occurred in a large stalag of ten thousand men. After we had been there a couple of weeks, my Anglican colleague preached to a large congregation. His first words were, "As I preach to you this morning, I want to say a word or two on a filthy and disgusting subject." You could have heard a pin drop. Then, to the men's surprise, he launched into a denunciation of certain rackets in the camp whereby those in charge of distributing food were taking a rake-off in camp marks, or even wedding rings, in exchange for extra rations. Remembering that, I began to have second thoughts about keeping a sermon aloof from all such mundane but morally loaded matters.

I was not going to be allowed to escape this dilemma as my ministry moved forward into the sixties and the battles raged first over civil rights and then the Vietnam War. It was always possible to continue expounding the Gospel with an emphasis on historic doctrines and individual morality. But I became increasingly aware that the policy of avoiding reference to current ethical controversies and political events was wrong for at least two reasons. One is that such preaching is never truly "neutral." It inevitably leaves the impression that one is supporting the status quo. A preacher in the sixties who said nothing about civil rights would be assumed to be on the side of leaving things alone. If he ignored the Vietnam War, he was really making a political statement in its support. The second reason for rejecting a policy of silence is theological. The doctrine of the Incarnation insists that "the Word was made flesh, and dwelt among us." This Word must then address every aspect of our common life "in the flesh," and not be isolated in some spiritual realm. In the Old Testament, the prophets continually invaded the political realm by pronouncing judgments on both domestic conditions, such as the plight of the poor, and foreign policy. Jesus seems to have avoided aligning himself with any political movement, but he did not hesitate to attack corruption and oppression. John the Baptist was consistently as outspoken and down-to-earth, whether he was relaying the Word of God to religious leaders, tax collectors, Roman soldiers, or the common people.

A few years ago, another pastor in the neighborhood and I had dinner with a well-known television preacher. We gave him a hard time about his statement that a successful preacher should never say anything controversial, confronting him with these examples from the Scriptures. He was receptive to our criticisms, but he made the point that, having attracted the crowds by avoiding controversy, one could then draft them into smaller groups to discover what a Christian must say on public, social, and political issues. It was a skillful defense, but the other pastor and I were not satisfied—and neither, I think, was he.

As I listened to occasional suggestions (I wish more were aware of how valuable suggestions are to a sensitive preacher), I began to realize that my congregation expected rather more reference to current affairs than I had been giving them. I had, in fact, been neglecting that other hand in Karl Barth's image of the preacher, the one with the morning newspaper. Talks with journalists underlined this lesson. It was clear that for them the Good News is not news unless it makes contact with what is actually going on in this world. I was shaken when an American preacher told me he had read a volume of sermons by a Scottish preacher whom we both admired, and he was astonished to find by the date on the flyleaf that they had been delivered in the midst of World War II. Nothing in the sermons referred to these tremendous events. I was sure that the Scottish preacher, who also conducted the prayers and was a devoted pastor, had the war very much in mind, but the American preacher's comment haunted me nonetheless. I became more sure than ever that a sermon is a contemporary event, and that there is no all-purpose sermon, equally preachable in the twenties or the eighties. (There is, I may add, an all-purpose sermon title which I have seen again and again—"For Such a Time as This"!)

What I had not resolved—and still haven't—is the question of *how* a preacher is to relate the Word to the morning newspaper. I have wrestled with this question; I have prayed about it; I have discussed it with a great variety of preachers and theologians. And still I have found no simple, all-encompassing answer. Perhaps this particular grace has not been given me. As you will note, I have rejected the easy solution of avoiding social and political topics altogether. But I am also conscious of the other extreme—the kind of preaching that is almost indistinguishable from a political party diatribe. Over the years I have evolved certain guidelines which I offer not as the oracles of an elderly apostle of the *via media* in this matter, but as an indication of some principles that have guided me, rightly or wrongly, during these last thirty years.

The first is never to ignore whatever is going on that raises acute ethical questions for a Christian, whether or not I have a specific proposal to endorse. I dislike the clumsy expression "consciousness-raising," but I suppose that is what I have been after. In the early sixties it seemed to me that in a church like ours, which strives to be class- and color-blind but tends to reflect the neighborhood in which it stands, it was necessary to address the subject of the glaring injustices that had chronically afflicted our society. In this particular instance we took action through the session in support of the Civil Rights Act, and others acted according to their conscience by participating in protest marches and demonstrations. In the seventies, although I never devoted an entire sermon to the theme of the Vietnam War (for reasons that follow), I tried to be sensitive to this horror and stir up concern as to how it could be brought to an end. On one occasion (it was the time of the so-called Christmas bombing), I supplied worshipers with paper and envelopes with which to write to the president. I prefer this method to asking people to sign something with which they may not completely agree. In the eighties, I have tried to keep the subject of abortion alive in our minds with references to the Christian conviction about the value of human life.

I am aware that this indirect method of referring to highly controversial questions leaves many unsatisfied. They may at times feel like saying, "Oh, come off it! Just let us know where you stand." My defense is simply that for me the preacher is not a free agent, an orator who simply speaks his mind on any topic whatever. He is bound by the Word he is charged to deliver in the name of Christ, and he seeks the guidance of the Spirit as he preaches. Therefore, opinions that I would feel free to express to anyone in ordinary conversation or set forth in a book like this are not necessarily those that I can voice as being what I believe to be the Word of God. However, in the sixties I did respond to the popular desire to know what I really thought about a lot of highly controversial subjects by offering a series of Lenten lectures in which I gave my frank opinions on a rich variety of subjects from war to divorce.

Another guideline that I have tried to follow is to ask myself what I would actually do about certain critical situations if I were president of the United States. If that sounds a little pompous, let me say that I commend this exercise to all who are tempted to sound off with simple solutions to very complicated questions of policy. When a nation is deeply involved, as we were at that time, in a war that many were convinced was morally and even strategically wrong, nothing is easier than to proclaim from the pulpit that we must immediately withdraw. I remember asking a bishop who had been making just that proclamation what exactly he proposed we should do. "Just get out," he said. "That's all." I then asked if he had ever seen an army in retreat that consequently suffered heavy casualties and endangered allies and the civilian population. I know that every government tries to muzzle criticism of its politics by using the old device of "If you only knew what I know." One of my professors in Edinburgh was Moderator during the time of the Italian-Abyssinian War. Most of us were disgusted by our government's lack of clear condemnation of the Italian action, and the Church had been quite outspoken. Our Moderator set off for London, and when he returned he gave us the "inside information" he had gotten from the Foreign Office, which was designed to moderate our criticism. It didn't—and in that case I think we were right. Still, it seems to me a useful exercise to put oneself in the shoes of the actual decision-maker before one shouts too confidently from the pulpit. To use a more contemporary illustration, let me take the case of abortion. I am opposed to abortion except in certain circumstances, and I was shocked by the decision of the Supreme Court legitimizing abortion on demand—and even more by our General Assembly's support of this position. But when I asked myself what I would have done if I had been in the president's shoes at this time, I realized that I would not have tried to turn the clock back to make all abortions illegal, remembering the hideous practical consequences of that position.

The next guideline that I have tried to follow on both sides of the Atlantic is "No *party* politics from the pulpit." I believe that during elections a preacher should declare the Christian's duty to exercise the right to vote. This seemed more necessary than ever when I discovered the shockingly low level of voter participation in the United States. I also think that a church should be willing to provide a forum in which speakers from different parties can present their case in an atmosphere of Christian concern, and I hope that we can develop this in my own church in the years ahead. I am not hesitant to reveal my own political preferences (or prejudices, as some would call them) in private conversation or at dinner parties, but I try my utmost not to let them intrude into a sermon. In the first place, it seems to me unfair to use the pulpit as a privileged platform (where rebuttal is seldom possible) to advocate one particular party's program. In the second place, to do so—especially in a church like mine, which is usually split down the middle in any presidential election—is to risk so alienating one half of the congregation that it will hear little of the Word of God.

Even this guideline, however, is difficult to absolutize. In Germany during the thirties, for example, a pastor who publicly condemned certain doctrines of the Nazis, as was clearly done in the Barmen Declaration, could be accused of playing party politics. And since coming to America, I have had to reckon with the fact that most black preachers have no inhibitions about supporting or attacking specific parties and candidates from the pulpit. It took me a little time to understand the historical roots of this tradition—the blunt fact that for years the Church was the only place where blacks could express their political aspirations, and the preacher was the main voice in the struggle for freedom. I could not help remembering that in my native land John Knox was hardly neutral as he thundered from the pulpit of St. Giles' against the policies of Mary, Queen of Scots. That tragic figure is now almost universally romanticized, but when Knox spoke of Jezebel, his congregations knew whom he meant.

I've spent some time on this well-worn theme of religion and politics not because my first years in an American pulpit were dominated by it, but because it still remains a sensitive question in this country. What puzzled me at first was the contradiction between the notion of a wall of separation between Church and State and the widespread recognition of the place of religion in American life. Are there not chaplains in Congress and in the armed forces, paid for by the State; and isn't this country unique among Western nations in still having a religious understanding of its origin and destiny? Can religion be totally banned from the system of education in a country such as this, so that children are educated in all disciplines except the one that has made the greatest mark on our civilization? Even on the secular level, what a fearful loss there is in the field of English literature, not to mention the rhythms of our common speech, when a generation is raised in total ignorance of the King James Bible.

During these years of my apprenticeship as an American preacher, I was not rethinking the "morning newspaper" aspect of preaching primarily in terms of politics, but much more in terms of a true pastoral relationship with those to whom I was speaking. I have noted the difficulty I had in understanding a postwar suburban congregation after years of preaching to my intimates in the prison camps. I had to make the same adjustment, in a minor way, as I came to know my congregation of New Yorkers. One of the joys of some thirty years of preaching at Madison Avenue has been the increasing sense of rapport that has developed between me and my congregation, despite its great diversity and its constantly changing membership. Only a preacher knows the contribution of the listeners to any sermon, and I have been immensely helped in my task by a responsive and alert congregation, and the knowledge that the prayers of many have been with me. There are, of course, disadvantages in a really long ministry—chiefly what I have mentioned already: a lack of variety in the understanding of the Gospel. However, I am not convinced that the present trend toward pastorates of four or five years is a good one. If I were a layperson, I think I would prefer a church where the minister stayed and the congregation kept changing rather than the other way around.

In this situation I have been blessed with colleagues who, despite having to listen to the same preacher for weeks at a time, often twice a Sunday, have been unfailingly loyal and most helpful in reminding an occasionally forgetful preacher which names are to be attached to which faces—and other such invaluable aids in the impossible task of getting to know about two thousand people. (Being no mathematician, I have always been puzzled by the fact that there are quite a few members here today who were attending Madison Avenue when I arrived in 1956. According to my calculations, if we lose roughly a hundred members a year and take in the same number, there should be none at all.) As it happens, the period immediately after the service is the time when I am poorest at remembering things that I ought to remember. My worst moment came when I inquired solicitously about the health of a member I had been visiting regularly, only to be told by his widow, "You buried him last Thursday." Luckily, she had a sense of humor—which is almost the most important "grace given" to either preacher or member of a Christian church. (Incidentally, what makes preaching to one's own so much more joyful than preaching to strangers is that they know when a remark is not meant to be taken seriously.)

Old ministers in Scotland used to warn me, "You can't please everybody, and there's something wrong if you do." Americans, as I have already noted, are far more apt to express appreciation than Scots, but I remember one shrewd critic telling me how he had listened to the opening of one of George Buttrick's sermons and had said to himself, "Nonsense!" He then looked keenly at me and said, "It's not a bad idea to arouse that reaction from time to time." I confess that I sometimes wonder whether strong approval of a sermon means just that the hearer thereof happened to strongly agree with it. I suppose what every preacher would like to hear is "I totally disagreed with you to begin with, but in the end you won me over," or even "I think you're wrong, but anyway, you made me think."

One of the most vital relationships for a preacher is that with the church organist and choirmaster. I have been fortunate to have the friendship and support of more than one organist in my ministry, and at present I revel in my collaboration with John Weaver, a superb musician and dedicated churchman. Even when my habits of preparation do not allow me to let him know the theme of the sermon in time for choir prac-

81

tices, we seem to have the mysterious ability to read each other's minds. Especially memorable services during these years have usually been ones in which music has played a big part.

Apart from such events as the celebration of a church anniversary or the successful conclusion of a fund drive, certain occasions stick in my memory. In 1964 we were the host church for the funeral of Mayor Wagner's first wife, who was a Presbyterian. We had to allow for the presence of an overflow congregation and a large number of distinguished figures from the political world—including, at the last moment, President Johnson, who had been in office only a few weeks since the assassination of President Kennedy. Under the circumstances, the security arrangements had to be thorough, and the church was sealed off and kept lit all night before the service. Admission was limited: only those who had received a telegram from the mayor could attend. One detail I remember particularly well. A representative of the fire department asked me somewhat aggressively, "You say your church can hold a thousand people. When was the last time a thousand were here?" And I had the pleasure of replying, "Last Sunday morning." Among the prominent guests at the service was Cardinal Spellman, who graciously invited me to join him in the closing prayers after the interment at the Roman Catholic cemetery in Brooklyn.

Another memorable service was that for Henry Luce, a devoted member of the church. The sanctuary was filled, of course, not only with our members but with many distinguished figures in politics and journalism. The service was relayed to the staff gathered in the Time/Life Building, and it had many repercussions for those who knew and admired this extraordinary man. I remember that he never failed to be in his pew when he was in New York, and even when he was traveling, he kept in touch. Just a week before his sudden death, he phoned me from somewhere in the Midwest on his way to Hawaii. As usual, he wasted no time on trivialities. "Did you preach recently on a text about a serpent on a rock?" he asked.

I thought fast, and it came back to me. "Yes, a sermon on wonder," I said, "based on two verses in Proverbs: 'There be three things which are too wonderful for me, yea, four which I know not: the way of an eagle in the air; the way of a serpent upon a rock; the way of a ship in the midst of the sea; and the way of a man with a maid.' "

"Thanks," he said. "I missed it, but I heard about it. Goodbye." I never dreamed this was to be our last conversation.

In the sixties we kept the old schedule, holding one service at 11:00 in the morning and another at 8:00 at night. During Lent the morning service was crammed, the congregation overflowing into our chapel. The people represented a cross-section of the neighborhood, which in those days included an extraordinary variety of occupations and ethnic backgrounds, everything from houses on Fifth and Park to blocks of walk-up apartments near the East River. The evening service, originally designed for those whose domestic duties kept them from the morning service, was by this time mainly attended by members of the Twenty-Thirty Club and their friends. This young adult group, originated by Frank Grebe, was extremely lively at this time. They met for serious discussion before the service on Sunday evening; arranged Bible studies, excursions, theater parties, and social work; and occasionally produced original, high-quality musicals written and scored by the members themselves. As we moved into the seventies, the changing pattern of our church life led the Session to institute morning services at 9:30 and 11:15, and, because of the gradually diminishing attendance at night, to abolish the evening service. (I think that the fate of evening services, both in Scotland and the United States, was largely determined by television and by the reluctance of many to walk the streets at night.) At this time there was one other Presbyterian church in New York that had an evening service, but I am told they abandoned it after I told the following story at a Presbytery dinner. A group of Edinburgh clergy were discussing what they called "the problem of the second service" when one of them announced he had solved it. He was asked how. "I abandoned it," he said simply. When he was asked what his elders had to say about that, he replied, "So far, none of them have noticed."

Shortly after I had settled in at Madison Avenue, it became clear that we were in for a period of social change and considerable unrest. What seemed to me an almost Edwardian pattern of life, with its social conventions, class distinctions, and widespread religiosity, was disintegrating. I don't claim to have foreseen the impact of the "Now" generation, with its flower children, its questioning of all traditions, its demonstrations and violent protests, its racial riots and tragic assassinations, but I sensed that something new was in the air and that my ministry would not continue with the comfortable assumptions of the fifties. It was a trying time for those who attempted to hold middle-of-the-road positions—to sympathize with the demands for change yet remember that the Church was not born yesterday and had some inherited wisdom that would be needed in the new age. Something also told me that this revolutionary period would probably be followed by a vigorous reaction. I remembered Dean Inge's remark that the one who marries the spirit of the age is soon likely to be widowed. Therefore, I was determined to listen to what the "Now" generation was saying. I appreciated what they were doing to expose shams and hypocrisies and was aware that much church activity must seem enslaved to past conventions, yet I was not prepared to throw overboard all traditions and forms of worship that had stood the test of time. (As I watched extremes of violence being used in the name of peace, I realized that hypocrisy is not the exclusive sign of an older generation.) The middle of the road—to which I am, by temperament, always "overdrawn"—is not necessarily the most comfortable position for a preacher. In those days it was easier to align oneself with one extreme or the other, and it still is. Both the rock-hewn conservative and the flaming liberal can attract an enthusiastic audience. The danger of the middle of the road is that it can lack the fire and the passion which are surely part of the Gospel we are called to proclaim. So the preacher in this position is vulnerable to the quip about "the bland leading the bland."

In those revolutionary days the Church naturally came under fire as part of "the establishment," and seminarians and many ministers were in the forefront of the attack. On one occasion, when I was paying my annual visit to preach at Harvard, the situation was such that the chaplain suggested that I confine myself to reading a lesson while he tried to utter some calming words. I was told that the service was likely to be interrupted (not an uncommon phenomenon in those days) by—of all groups—the Divinity School. Nothing untoward did in fact happen, but I had a taste of what criticisms were being directed at the Church. I had a similar experience when I was asked to speak at an open-air meeting on the campus at Columbia. As it was a long time since I had been challenged to present the Gospel without the conventional barricades of pulpit or platform and a quietly responsive audience, I accepted the invitation. And in the end I met with little opposition and no violence—despite the waiting ambulances.

This was a time when churches like mine were being told not only by seminarians but also by popular theologians that the day of the old church-on-the-corner was over. The new Church would be dispersed into "the real world," and "experimental ministries" were the wave of the future. Sermons were being dismissed as mere "God-talk." I could not help remarking at times that it was the old church-on-the-corner that kept the seminaries in existence, and that, while I am all for "experimental ministries," there is no sign anywhere that they are replacing the worship and activities of the parish church with all its barnacles. As for "God-talk"—this was the period when some of the radicals proceeded to talk God to death. It was about this time that I noticed how the fundamentalism of the right, which corrupts the Gospel with its obscurantism and fanatical dogmatism, can be paralleled by the fundamentalism of the left. Once, when I was asked if I didn't feel afraid to denounce the Vietnam War in a church on Madison Avenue, I answered that I felt no such constraint, but that I might well be afraid to defend the war at Union Seminary. It was at this time that the sermon class I had inherited from George Buttrick was discontinued because of lack of interest in homiletics. Colleagues of mine who had also been teaching such a course had gradually stopped, and my own class shrank to four, so clearly the time had come to close down. I am glad to note that now, in the eighties, homiletics at Union is alive and well.

It was becoming evident that we were not going to be immune to change at Madison Avenue, nor did I want us to be. Clubs and associations of the old style—with their president, secretary, and treasurer, and regular programs with an obligatory speaker—were on the way out. The Twenty-Thirty Club dwindled for various reasons, and it was later replaced by a less structured young-adult group. The Women's Association, the Business and Professional Women's Club, and other traditional groups went out of business—but never with the idea that we should just forget about the need for people to get together as Christians to get to know one another better than contact at Sunday worship allows and to share in discussions based on common interests. A men's group, for instance, sprang into being with no formal organization at all. It grew to include about a hundred members who met in different homes and talked about the faith. Other discussion and prayer groups have also come and gone. We have also tried to convert the numerous committees of the church into spiritual communities (you see how desperately I try to avoid the word "fellowship") rather than business meetings preceded by a prayer.

These are some of the things that were making their impact on me as I responded to the grace that was given to me to adjust to a new church and a new country. Increasingly I felt at home as a preacher in America and in love with my congregation and even, at times, with New York City. (I now find myself forestalling the usual remark about this city by saying, "I love living in New York, but I'd hate to visit it," which simply means that, although I now know as well as anybody the many things that are wrong with it, there is nowhere else that I want to live.) Outside my congregation, I was being drawn into activities that enlarged my understanding of religion in America, opened my mind to traditions that were foreign to me, and enriched me with friendships among men and women of other faiths or of none. It surprised me to find how soon I was accepted in this city—not as a foreign voice but as a representative New Yorker. During times of crisis, such as the tragic assassinations of John and Robert Kennedy and Martin Luther King, Jr., I often had to dash to a studio to speak for a few minutes on TV. My old friend radio also came back into the picture, and I found another outlet as evangelist and pastor. On one occasion I was leaving on vacation and had taken possession of a cabin on the old *United States*. I had just settled in with the delightful thought "No more meetings or phone calls for at least five days" when a phone in the cabin began to ring. A kindly voice was inviting me to succeed Ralph Sockman on the "National Radio Pulpit." At that time the program had a much wider circulation and influence than it does today, when the networks are not falling over themselves to give airtime to such religious programs, and I sat on the bed thinking again about what God was up to in transplanting me to this country.

That naturally brought up a question I had been shelving. If this was now my parish—and, at my age, it was likely to be the final one—was it not time that I became an American citizen? Two things were holding me back. The first was the reluctance, which is shared by the British and the French particularly, to give up old loyalties and assume new ones. But this faded when I learned that the emphasis in the naturalization process is not on the abandonment of old traditions but on the bringing of them into this amazing community of immigrants. I also felt a growing need to identify myself with those for whom I was preacher and pastor. The words of Ruth are appropriate. No one was "intreating me to leave," and my response was, "Where thou lodgest, I will lodge: thy people shall be my people, and thy God my God." The other source of my delay in taking this step is much more mundane. I am allergic to filling out forms—and you should see what is required by the immigration authorities. One question concerned the clubs of which I had been a member. Since my record went back to the Literary and Debating Society of my high school and ran on to dozens of clubs (including the Golfing Society of Oflag IX A/H at Spangenberg), I was baffled until I learned that this hurdle could be crossed by the expedient of scrawling "no political parties" across the space. More sinister was the question "Have you committed adultery since coming to the United States?" A British friend who had been through this procedure told me he had phoned the authorities about this question. "Is it really necessary?" he inquired.

Eventually I joined a fascinating group of people from all over the world and duly swore allegiance to the United States of America, like millions of Scots before me. And imported Scotch, I like to say, after some thirty years ought to be mature.

Chapter Six

IMPRESSIONS
AND
ADJUSTMENTS

One thing that I noticed about America during those first decades of my new ministry was a passion for self-analysis. At first it seemed odd to me that churches, for instance, should be continually asking what their purpose was and how they were fulfilling it. In Scotland it was assumed that everybody knew what a church was for, and nobody could be bothered with that kind of question raised in the process of self-exam-ination. Since the weight of tradition was felt much less over here, the churches showed no reluctance in applying business techniques to their work—goal-setting, market research, and salesmanship. At first I found the self-scrutiny of American churches disturbing, and then I began to wonder if the churches in the old country didn't need to be disturbed, for each time I returned to Great Britain, I was struck anew by the contrast between the liveliness of American churches and the rigidity and torpor of much British church life. I still believe that self-examination and introspection have in recent years been over-emphasized in the United States and can indicate a lack of self-confidence in both Church and State. Nevertheless, I have found it good spiritual discipline to be forced now and then to think back to the basics, and I am grateful for the American layman who keeps asking awkward questions.

What is not so helpful is a disease that I call "the paralysis of analysis." We are tempted to think that the setting up of a committee to deal with an urgent problem means that we are on the way to a solution, and that discussion can be a substitute for action. When I think, for instance, of the enormous number of reports on evangelism that have been issued by the mainline churches, and the surveys that have been done by individual churches, I can't help reflecting on the Church of the Book of the Acts, which, with a minimum of analysis and discussion, got on with the job of evangelism with spectacular results. I think too of the hours spent in devising ways of performing the pastoral work of a church. Once, when ministers here had been working for months on various plans for parish visitation, somebody finally said at a meeting, "Why don't we stop all this and go visit someone?"

The obsession with analysis has also led to the institutionalizing (a horrible word for a horrible phenomenon) of what used to be called "the cure of souls" and is now referred to everywhere as "pastoral counseling." What used to be the natural instinct of a church member to consult a minister in a time of trouble or confusion has been elevated to a pseudo-science complete with the associated jargon. To me there is something dehumanizing about all this, but I have to confess that I have not solved the question of how to be available on a regular basis for consultation, or how to break down the terrible image of the preacher in a big church as being too busy to talk privately with any of his flock. (Incidentally, I have found that, while church members are almost oversensitive to the pressures on a minister's time, those with no connection at all to the church think nothing of spending hours, in person or on the telephone, expounding their problems.)

During these years, I was being molded by my new environment, learning more about the people to whom I was called to communicate the Gospel, studying the "morning newspaper," and adapting to the ideals of efficiency and order that are so much a part of the vitality of the American Church. While all this was going on, what was happening to my own understanding of the Christian Gospel, to my theology, and to my contacts with and attitude toward other faiths—particularly the Roman Catholic Church and the Jewish community?

My new experiences in the area of ecumenical and Christian-Jewish relations were so challenging and mind-expanding that I must devote a later chapter to this subject. At the moment, I want to think back on the effect that the first twenty years of my New York ministry had on my call to preach "the unsearchable riches of Christ to the Gentiles"—that is, the unbelievers.

These years taught me that, although there was a great deal of popular religion around and the clergy were regarded with benevolent respect (while slipping a little on the social totem-pole), a great segment of academia and of the opinion-makers in the land seemed almost totally alienated from the traditional Christianity of the creeds. Much popular religion was being tolerated for its therapeutic value but was intellectually scorned, and the fundamentalist fringe, as it was then considered, was generally ignored. What was missing were strong voices and vibrant worship representing the historic denominations and what the creed calls "the holy catholic Church."

A Reinhold Niebuhr might shock academia with his thesis on the relevance of the doctrine of original sin to political judgments. A Fulton Sheen might demonstrate that orthodox Christianity could on occasion be made intellectually as well as emotionally satisfying. But, on the whole, the Christian Gospel was not doing well among the clash of philosophies competing for the ear of thinking people at a critical moment in the country's history. I had no illusions that I had arrived on the scene "for such a time as this" (to quote the all-purpose sermon title), but I did hope to play a modest part in evangelism of this kind. Therefore, I decided that I would do my part as a preacher by taking the risk of being accused of talking over people's heads rather than of talking down to them. As the seventies, with their reaction to the activism of the sixties, slipped into the eighties, there were signs of a hankering after the historic faith and a hunger for a worship that was not born yesterday yet offered unashamedly the dimension of the supernatural. (For the theologians of the sixties, "supernatural" was a dirty word.) The difference now was that, while the activist wing of the Church was losing ground and impact on society, the fundamentalist fringe was becoming a religious power to be reckoned with and, surprisingly, a new political force.

Before this becomes the kind of analysis I have been deploring, let me return to my story and recall some incidents in which I, consciously or unconsciously, experienced the grace of God at work. There was the area of radio and TV, which has always seemed to me one of God's great gifts to the Church that has scarcely been recognized. What would Saint Paul have given for the opportunity to enter a million homes and talk intimately about Christ to whoever was watching or listening! Yet, on the whole, the historic churches had done little to evangelize in this way, leaving religion on the air in the hands of charismatic personalities or hard-boiled fanatics. No church seemed willing to spend the vast sums of money required to launch radio and television ministries, although I can think of other directions in which lavish sums were flowing during these years. For me this ministry has two primary functions: one is to offer the elderly and the housebound a living contact with the Church; the other is to catch the ear of the unbeliever or seeker with the challenge of the Gospel. What it cannot and ought not to be is a radio or television church. There is no such thing. This ministry is the handmaid of the Church Catholic and not an alternative denomination—which it is in some danger of becoming.

Letters from viewers and listeners give some indication of the fulfillment of the two aims described. The majority of these letters are moving expressions of what it means for lonely, elderly, and confined people to have this contact with the Word of God in sermon form. In my first efforts at radio preaching, I tried to cultivate a simple, popular style in imitation of preachers who had that knack, but I learned that the average listener is not really different from those a preacher hopes to find in the pew, and that it is always a mistake to force myself into a mold that God did not make for me. From time to time I get a letter that says something like, "I was twiddling the dial when I heard a religious program announced. I was about to switch it off when something you said caught my attention"; then it goes on to raise real questions of belief and invite further correspondence. Obviously, such a ministry could be expanded if we were training men and women who have a gift for communicating on the air and who could devote themselves full-time to the follow-up work that would be involved. I still think that this is one of the neglected means of grace.

The question of reaching the nonreligious or skeptical audience by means of the printed word runs into the same difficulties. Articles on religious books are published by religious companies and find their way into religious bookstores. So the dialogue between the believer and the unbeliever is apt to be throttled before it really gets started. What I would like to see in this country is a massive effort to present Christian convictions through books that avoid religious clichés, have literary merit, and at the same time are faithful to the historic Gospel; through articles that infiltrate the secular press; through plays, movies, and TV documentaries that are first-class productions presenting a Christian point of view. We need to wage a fresh assault on those whom Schleiermacher in the nineteenth century called "the cultured despisers of religion."

Behind such an enterprise there has to be a strong and stimulating theology. I've been trying to think of the theological currents that have affected me since I settled in the United States. The trouble with preachers who assume the responsibility of a large city church is that the time for serious reading becomes more and more limited. It will be obvious to the discerning that I have to a great extent lived on theological capital I acquired in the thirties and forties, but I do try to keep abreast through periodicals, lectures, and friendships in the theological world. I also make an effort to read one or two solid works during my summer break. (I remember deciding twenty years ago that it was time that I tried to understand what Paul Tillich was saying to that generation, and I succeeded in reading and marking, if not inwardly digesting, his *Dogmatics* on a round-trip freighter voyage to Europe. What I got out of the book was chiefly an understanding of his attempts at bridge-building between the Gospel and contemporary culture. It was that concern that led me to my long association with the Society for the Arts, Religion and Contemporary Culture, which has had a precarious but lively existence over these years.)

I don't think it is simply the nostalgia of the elderly that leads me to remark on the lack of great theological figures on the landscape of the English-speaking world during these years. It has been the era of little books and ephemeral controversies. Many will remember the uproar caused by Bishop Robinson's *Honest to God,* and the even more ephemeral hubbub aroused by "the theology of the Death of God," which is what William Buckley would call an oxymoron—a contradiction in terms. Harvey Cox keeps the kettle boiling with a succession of stimulating books, serving up everything from a celebration of "the Secular City" to invitations to find our way back to the Transcendent. Like many other Protestants, I found myself turning for solid fare to Roman Catholic scholars like Karl Rahner, Hans Küng, Edward Schillebeeckx, and—especially in the field of biblical commentary—Raymond Brown. This is not to say that no serious theology is going on in our seminaries and that no solid works of scholarship are being produced. Take these comments as the ill-informed judgments of an overbusy preacher in whose veins run the memories of giants now deceased.

If there seemed to be little time for serious reading, there was certainly even less for writing. I arrived in this country with books that I had already published, and since then have added to the record. That sounds enormously impressive until you realize that many of them required no special writing because they were collections of sermons which my efficient secretary simply bundled up and dispatched to the publisher. Since the demand for volumes of sermons is not excessive, there were, of course, other works which I wrote for a specific purpose—the Lyman Beecher Lectures on preaching, the Gunning Lectures on "Christian Ethics," a brief commentary for the TEV version of Paul's epistles, and a book on evangelism. I also made an attempt to reach the nonchurch public with *The Faith Is Still There.* Breaking that barrier is extremely difficult, but my prayer is that some American writer will appear who will be able to do for this generation what C. S. Lewis did so spectacularly in his day. In my opinion, the author who comes nearest to doing just that is my friend Frederick Buechner, who has the gift of making novels subtly Christian and theology funny. When I am asked how I find time for the writing business, I have to reply that I can write only when I am extremely busy. None of my books has been composed during a leisurely summer vacation.

It is impossible to look back on the last few decades without taking into account the revolution that is occurring with the arrival of women as ordained ministers, theologians, and church leaders. In my early days in the ministry, there were always some women in the pulpit, and many, of course, whose writings were influential. But I hope that by now we have reached the stage when such a feminine input is no longer regarded as exceptional and somewhat odd. Unfortunately, we have not quite reached the stage at which the full potential of the feminine contribution to the life and thinking of the Church can be realized. Centuries of male dominance in the Church have left their mark. During these last twenty years or so, I have noticed the barriers that have slowly been coming down, and the more obvious examples of male prejudice—no, let me simply say prejudice, as there is, in my experience, at least as much resistance to the prominence of women in the Church among women of the laity as among men. But what has been most striking is the persistence of certain assumptions that are part of a male preacher's excess baggage from the past, including certain stereotypes of the role of women in the Christian community. These are reflected obnoxiously in a considerable number of hymns. I am not fond of the practice of announcing hymns with the addendum "omitting verses so-and-so," but on one occasion recently I selected the hymn "Rejoice, Ye Pure in Heart" and noted in the bulletin "Omit verse 2." At the forum after the service, a young girl asked me why this verse had been dropped. I replied, "Do you think of yourself as a maiden meek?"—for that is part of the offensive line: "strong men, and maidens meek." In my earlier days as a preacher, it would never even have occurred to me to question such a phrase, nor the habit of constantly using masculine pronouns. Once, about ten years ago, I began drafting a sermon and found myself writing "If a modern historical novelist was describing this scene, *he* would . . ."—and then it dawned on me that the great majority of modern historical novelists are women.

This raises the question that is agitating the seminaries today (though not, my guess is, bestirring the average congregation) concerning what is called "sexist language," especially in prayers and in the Bible. I am sympathetic to this concern, and I try to be aware of the traps into which a traditionalist like me can fall. But I do draw a distinction between the totally unnecessary use of masculine pronouns (for example, in the General Thanksgiving the phrase "all men" can easily, if perhaps not quite rhythmically, become simply "all," and on many occasions "man" can be changed, with linguistic accuracy, to "they") and the radical shredding of Scripture involved in a determined attempt to eliminate all masculine language, even such as refers to the plain fact that our Lord was a man. I am not only concerned about some of the theological implications of extreme desexing of this kind but confess to having certain aesthetic sensibilities that are violated by such practice. I loathe the word "person" as a substitute for "men and women." It seems the most *impersonal* way of referring to a human being. Recently I heard of an ardent feminist called upon to read the story of the feeding of the multitude. When she came to Matthew's statement "They that did eat were about five thousand men," on the spur of the moment she changed "men" to "persons"—only to find that she had to continue with the phrase "beside women and children." I am sure that a great deal of work remains to be done on this question of language and that, with sensitivity and common sense, a quiet revolution will occur. As in all changes that agitate the Church from time to time, the enlightenment of the Holy Spirit will not be quenched by the excesses of the fanatic.

Even if there had been no feminist movement during these years, the language problem would have been with us. It was one I had to wrestle with from the beginning of my American ministry. What version of Scripture should be used in the late twentieth century? What kind of language is suitable for public prayer? When I left Scotland, the use of the King James Version was still almost automatic. Everyone was familiar with it. It was taught in the public schools, used on all national religious occasions like a coronation, and, of course, saturated our literature with its rhythms and cadences. But we preachers were beginning to get restless with some of the conventional language of the prayers to be found in the Book of Common Order (from which our Book of Common Worship was derived). To coin a phrase, it was a bit too "vouchsafey." We were searching for a style that would be less dated and yet retained a dignity and rhythm suitable for public worship.

There is one great advantage in the universal use of a particular translation of the Bible. It means that certain texts are absorbed by a great variety of people in identical words, and that a preacher knows that his scriptural allusions are readily recognized. To this day it is still the King James Version that is universally recognized in the English-speaking world. Yet any intelligent traditionalist must admit that no version of Scripture is going to last forever. The King James itself was a fresh attempt at a translation when others were available and being debated. At seminary we were encouraged to use new translations, chiefly because they incorporated the vastly increased knowledge of linguistics and variant readings of the manuscript. As young preachers, we faced the problem of acquainting congregations with the more correct translations of familiar texts without constantly irritating them with the remark "The Greek here means something entirely different." I remember preaching a sermon on the magnificent text from Isaiah that in the King James Version reads, "When the enemy shall come in like a flood, the Spirit of the Lord shall lift up a standard against him." On doing my homework, I found that the Hebrew cannot possibly be twisted into meaning any such thing—in fact, the text is so corrupt that nobody knows what it means. Whether I explained all this to my flock at that time I can't recall. Today I think I might use the text, explaining the problem but adding that I see no reason why the Holy Spirit should not have inspired the translators of the King James Version!

When I arrived in America, I found that the Revised Standard Version had won almost universal acceptance in the mainline churches. (To this day, fundamentalists of a certain stripe remain faithful to the King James—perhaps for the reason said to have been given by one of them: "If it was good enough for Saint Paul, it's good enough for me.") The RSV was also being used in our church schools. Soon, however, the arrival of the New English Bible offered another alternative for public as well as private reading. It has been followed by a flood of versions, and it seems clear that no one of them is going to become the accepted version for our day.

My own practice has been to follow a rough rule whereby at least one of the three lessons in our normal order of worship will be from the King James. I still feel that it will be a great loss if a generation should be raised in the Church in total ignorance of a book that has had such an enormous influence on not only the religious formation but the literary heritage of the English-speaking peoples. For other readings I often use the New English Bible. It is clear and accurate, and has a literary quality that other recent translations notoriously lack. And people know it is a modern translation when they hear it; with the RSV they are apt to think they are listening to the King James and then are bothered by a sudden lapse from the familiar form of words.

The sixties and seventies were a period of liturgical upheaval in the major denominations of the Church, complicated by the fact that Vatican II had abruptly replaced medieval Latin with the vernacular in the Roman mass. Once again I found myself steering a course between a rigid traditionalism on the one hand and a surrender to passing fads on the other. If the language of the King James Bible and the prayers and ceremonies of the Book of Common Worship were becoming incomprehensible, even—to some—repugnant, then something had to be done. A living Church cannot be frozen into any particular pattern of either sixteenth-century Bible and prayers or nineteenth-century hymns. As I often have to remind those who ask why we can't always sing familiar hymns, there was a time when even "Jesus, Lover of My Soul" was sung for the first time—and there were certainly complaints about this "unfamiliar hymn," an indication that the language of public worship has often changed quite dramatically over the centuries. Yet I was not convinced that the time had come to jettison all familiar words and forms and yield to the current liturgy of guitars and balloons. With the aid of wise and sympathetic worship committees (an advisory body that didn't exist in Scotland), we managed to survive the sixties and emerge with a form of worship which is perhaps still too rigid but has been devised to "bring forth out of the treasure things new and old."

Among the many factors to be considered in wrestling with this question of language is one that has to a great extent determined my thinking. As I have indicated, I have found American church life immensely stimulating and lively compared with what I knew in the old country, but there is one element that seems weak if not entirely missing. It is difficult to put into words. Rudolf Otto used the word "numinous" to indicate what I mean. I am thinking of what we understand by "holy" when we use the word in its biblical sense. It refers to the dimension that we still can call "supernatural"—that which is beyond, transcendent, and evokes a sense of awe and wonder. That seems to me the missing note in American Protestantism. Children, even ultramodern children, have an instinctive sense of this—only too often it is rubbed out by those who are determined to eliminate the sense of mystery in religion, to explain everything, and thus to secularize the faith. I feel strongly that the sense of friendliness and welcome that should characterize Christian worship must be held in balance by a sense of the presence of the holy. After all, where else is this to be found in our secularized society? In this connection, I have discussed with a variety of people our continued use of the "thou" and "thee" when addressing the Deity. Admittedly, "thou" was, in the sixteenth century, a very intimate mode of address, similar to the French *tu* and the German *du*. But in English this usage disappeared, and "thou" was reserved for God. Thus, over the centuries, it has conveyed something of this sense of the holy, the transcendent, the numinous, which most would agree we can ill afford to lose. I am not rigid about this, and it may well be that since the Roman Church has adopted the vernacular and its use of "you," this usage will become universal. Meantime, I find it interesting that when this usage is discussed in a worship committee, it is today's teenagers who are most vociferous in preferring "thou."

As you can imagine, life for me in my new parish during the sixties and seventies was not chiefly devoted to questions of liturgical linguistics or even the feminist movement. I soon realized that the life of any church in New York, no matter how solid and settled it seems, is in fact extremely precarious. During this period, many were going out of business, even institutions that seemed well established. With others, we suffered the fluctuations in attendance, and even financial mini-crises now and then. In spite of the magnificent quality of the lay leadership and the team spirit among the ministers, Madison Avenue was no place for a preacher to sit back and devote himself entirely to the production of weekly sermons. I struggled with matters of administration in which, fortunately, I have always had colleagues more competent than I. I managed to understand budgets, even if it was only the bottom line. I found myself involved more than once in vast fund-raising campaigns which, by the grace of God, were encouragingly successful. I tried to keep in touch with the up-and-coming generation, even risking the insertion of a children's sermon in the 9:30 service. (I decided to undertake this practice—which a Scottish friend of mine once referred to as "a coy irrelevance" in worship—on the condition that it would always be directly related to the sermon of the day, be understandable to the children, and not last more than two or three minutes.) It has been good to hear the convictions and opinions of successive confirmation classes, which over the years have ranged from the conventional to the rebellious to the eager and convinced. My knowledge of New York's hospitals has become extensive, and it has been a joy to have the collaboration of the doctors in the congregation in this kind of pastoral care. Like many pastors, I have learned what prayer can mean at a bedside, or in a home, including at those moments when one wonders whether to offer it or not. I have discovered that the average American is less embarrassed by such prayers than some Scots. (It was one of our Scots members, no longer with us, who responded to my suggestion of a prayer with "All right—but keep it short!")

IMPRESSIONS AND ADJUSTMENTS

In keeping with my ordination vows, I have tried to be a dutiful presbyter, although I have little relish for still more committee work and no taste for church politics. When asked by a higher court to assume a certain responsibility, I don't feel free to refuse, but I have found them understanding of the constraints of time. For instance, I was asked to serve on the committee that produced the Confession of 1967, and I found the task extremely engrossing. But time pressures led me to resign, thus giving some opponents of the Confession the glad but false impression that I was opposed to the result. My stint as a commissioner to the General Assembly in 1968 was an education in the intricacies and organizational complexities of our denomination, and increased my admiration of those who have the necessary gifts of leadership and foresight. One committee of the Assembly on which I was glad to serve dealt with the question of "the gifts of the Spirit," with special reference to glossolalia, or speaking in tongues. The committee was a truly representative group of men and women, ranging from those who had the gift of glossolalia and saw it as a sign that the Spirit was moving toward the renewal of our churches, to experienced church officials who warned of such things as divisiveness and schism.

I shall have to say more about evangelism in this generation, but before I comment on the theory and practice of "making disciples" in this pluralist society, let me say a word or two about what has made these years at Madison Avenue so spiritually rich and mind-expanding. That means simply talking about individual people I have come to know. As I think back, the number of "most unforgettable characters" I have known grows more and more extensive. An autobiographer, however, is faced with the dilemma of selection—with the reminder, as he nears the present day, that most of the people he will mention are still alive, and with the question, if he is a pastor, as to what should be divulged and what warrants reticence. Protestant ministers are surely not altogether free from what our Catholic friends know as "the secrecy of the confessional." So, even if I disappoint any who might now be awaiting some spicy revelations or even some thrilling "now-it-can-be-told" stories, let me confine myself to one un-forgettable character who became a member of this church.

The story begins way back in 1943, in Oflag IX A/H in Spangenberg, Germany. I was then conducting a series of talks on the faith, later published as *Prisoners' Quest.* These were another of my attempts, already described, to communicate the Gospel, this time to senior officers with a good education and varied contact with the Church. A tremendous theological argument developed between believers and unbelievers, which over the months was fueled by the occasional arrival in the camp of a book dealing with religious questions. One such book aroused considerable interest. It was called *The Impor-tance of Living,* written by a Chinese philosopher and novelist called Lin Yutang. We heard that it was a best-seller in the English-speaking world, and when I got hold of it, I was de-lighted by the style, wit, and human gusto of the author. But I thought it unfortunate that it contained a sparkling chapter entitled "Why I Am a Pagan." Lin Yutang had been raised in a Christian family in China, but as a teenager he had decided that he had been deprived of the rich pagan heritage of his own country and so renounced the Christian faith. For our opponents in the theological debate that was raging in the camp, this was manna from heaven—though they would not have put it that way. Lin Yutang managed to poke fun at Chris-tian missionaries, track down inconsistencies in Christian be-lief and practice, and paint a most attractive picture of the dogma-free life of the pagan. It was all done, however, with such charm and elegance of style that I resolved to buy a copy of the book when and if I ever got home. Which I did.

I knew that Lin Yutang had written many other books and was still in full course as a novelist, but the postwar years I have described, which led to my transplanting in the United States, left little time for literary byways. But *The Importance of Living* was there among the other books that crossed the Atlantic with me. One afternoon in the late fifties, George Hood—a beloved colleague of mine who had spent some twenty years as a missionary in China and who as minister emeritus in our church was very active in looking after our large Chinese contingent—came to see me in my study. He explained that a Chinese couple wanted to become members, that the lady in question had been a churchgoer for many years but that her husband had abstained for about twenty years but was now coming to our Sunday services. George wondered if I would have a talk with him and see if he qualified for membership. "What's his name?" I asked. "Lin Yutang," said George, and wondered aloud why I should look so incredulous.

A few days later a shy and scholarly Chinese gentleman came to our apartment, looking vaguely apprehensive. We settled into chairs and exchanged the usual conversational gambits. Then I produced my pipe and filled it. At this, his face broke into a broad grin; he brought out his pipe and settled back, totally relaxed. He told me about his youthful revolt against Christianity and the development of his philosophical thinking, about his literary and academic career, and about his wife's efforts to get him to go to church with her. The consequences were sometimes disastrous: when they hit upon little "colonial" churches in various parts of the world, he would make mincemeat of the sermon after the service. But all the time he was revising his estimate of the place of Christianity in the struggle for the human soul in our generation, and was being steadily recaptured by the person of Christ himself. He had now been coming to Madison Avenue for about a year, he said. On the first occasion, it being All Saints' Sunday, I had been speaking about eternal life (of all things), and something—this grace given?—set him off on a new pilgrimage. He told me frankly what he believed and didn't believe, and then asked if he could be received into membership of our church. I was so moved by the story that I wanted to embrace him on the spot, but, as I remember, contented myself by saying, "Well, my own theology is a little more orthodox than yours, but I could probably say that about half my Session."

Y. T., as he liked to be called, and his wonderful wife, Hong, who wrote delightful books on Chinese cookery, became devoted and stimulating members of Madison Avenue, never missing a service unless they were off to take the sun in the Caribbean. Y. T. willingly spoke to church groups, and I interviewed him on TV. His next book was entitled *Pagan to Christian*. Unfortunately, it didn't make the stir it once might have—for two reasons. One was that those who thought of him as an ally in the cause of what is now known as "secular humanism" were disgusted by his change of mind. The other reason was that zealous evangelicals who thought that his would be a conventional story of conversion to their narrow concept of the Christian life were shocked by some of his casual remarks about smoking, drinking, and going to Parisian nightclubs. However, *Time* magazine gave the book a lively review, and Y. T. settled down to produce more books. The serious philosophic and historical ones he inscribed for me; what he called the "naughty novels" he gave to my wife. He was more than a writer. His genius ran to the invention not only of a Chinese typewriter but of a simple electric one that could be used with a single finger—a boon to the handicapped. Among his avocations was a passion for deep-sea fishing. I spent several nights with him rolling around in boats off Long Island.

About 1970 the Yutangs left for Taiwan. When I stopped there a few years later, on my way back from Australia, they entertained me splendidly. Y. T.'s energy never flagged until an illness led to his death in 1976. Before he left New York, he said to me one day, "My publisher has presented me with an enormous Bible. I don't know what to do with it. Can you use it in the church?" And that is the Bible that to this day you can see open on our communion table.

Chapter Seven

DON'T
LABEL ME,
PLEASE

One discovery I have made in this attempt to tell my tale in the light of the mysterious presence of the grace of God is that the closer I come to the present day, the more difficult it is to describe what has happened to me. In fact, when I come to the mid-eighties, the tale will inevitably fade away with, I hope, the assurance that "grace thus far" will take care of the rest here and hereafter. It is somehow easier to detect the pattern of God's interventions from the perspective of fifty years or so than from the vantage point of a few decades. Although the Bible warns us against living in the past, it does insist that we should not only press forward in faith but regularly glance backward in faith to realize the great actions of God in events that we did not understand at the time. Thus the Old Testament, which urges the people of God continually forward to the promised Kingdom, looks back in nearly every book to the story of the Exodus from Egypt, which at the time was merely one incident in the tumultuous story of slave revolts and tribal wanderings in the Middle East. In the same way, the rapidly expanding Church of the New Testament was rooted in the events of Calvary and Easter morning, which were trivial in the eyes of the Roman authorities involved but became more and more luminous in the memory of the disciples and the life of the Church.

Some might think that thirty years in one parish is long enough to offer a little perspective of this kind. But I am not finding it so. This isn't because 1956, when this wandering Scot settled in, signaled the end of a period of constant change and strange interventions in my plans. After all, it was by no means the obvious place in which to find the fulfillment of my ministry, my major contribution, so to speak, to the Church of Jesus Christ—my ultimate response to the call to preach and be a pastor, from which I had been so often wriggling away. "Grace thus far," yes, but how did I know that the abrupt change of pace and of environment and the general uprooting might not make the American adventure another brief one, or that once again the temptation would come to dodge the call to preach (as indeed it did). As it became more and more obvious to me over the years at Madison Avenue that this was going to be my lifework, the thought of moving dropped out of my mind, but that has not meant that the decades I have spent here represent a slice of time that can be neatly divided into decades which I can analyze in retrospect, or that this story can gracefully wind down with some septuagenarian reflections on lessons learned and "grace thus far." The real trouble I have in telling the tale of the last three decades is that it is too soon to see what was really happening, and that I still feel very much in the middle of it all.

At this point let me offer a footnote about "decades." There is no reason at all to suppose that history, even less the grace of God, pays any attention to our arbitrary way of counting the years. Preachers of my vintage are fond of talking glibly about "the sixties" or "the seventies" as if events and opinions neatly shifted gear every ten calendar years. It occurred to me recently that if we try to date some of the changes in people's thinking and their social, political, and religious attitudes, a much saner division would be mid-decade to mid-decade. In my recollection, 1955 to 1965 was a very different period from 1965 to 1975, and 1975 to 1985 was yet another. Looking back, I find that it was the rapid changes of the religious climate of these times which forced me to rethink theological positions, to decide how to respond to new challenges, and to seek the guidance of grace as to the direction and activities of a church like ours. Thirty years is too soon for real perspective. When we are on the job, one year seems very much like another, and it is only in retrospect that we can see that 1968, for instance, was a terrible year for the nation and a critical one for any church.

When I arrived in the United States at the beginning of 1956, I was not under any illusion that I was about to settle into a quiet haven where all I had to do was to work hard at the production of at least one sermon a week. In spite of the "Eisenhower boom" in religion, I found that the fashionable posture in the seminaries and the more liberal churches at this time was one of suspicion and disdain. "Superficial" was their word to describe the religious boom, and was the theme of a reported address by a noted theologian. ("Superficial," snorted one of our more opinionated members to me. "How the hell does he know it's superficial?") Perhaps the accusation was eventually borne out by the crime statistics, which seemed to be rising as fast, or faster, than church membership.

Anyway, I found myself—not for the first time—in the uncomfortable position of seeing both sides, and wishing that Americans didn't reach so quickly for labels to attach to every church and every preacher. I was glad to discover that my predecessors, George Buttrick and Henry Sloane Coffin, had not drawn upon themselves or our church a theological or social party label. Each was a man of strong, sometimes controversial convictions, but both stood for the proclamation and the living out of the historic Christian faith, and the centrality of worship in the life of the Church. I decided that it was possible to preach a Gospel with overtones of Karl Barth and Reinhold Niebuhr and with at least a flavor of the simplicity and directness of Billy Graham, and that while expounding the full range of biblical truth it was not necessary to denounce "the power of positive thinking." In a TV series called "Protestant Heritage" that I had been invited to conduct, I did a program on Niebuhr (with great trepidation, since I knew he would be watching). I tried to give some impression of what we owe to his insights into the meaning of the faith in the world of politics and international relations. At about the same time, I was encouraging my congregation to support the Billy

Graham campaign—not because I felt this was the one way to evangelize in our generation, nor because Billy's theology was identical with mine, but because I had gotten to know Billy in Scotland, and had great respect for his sincerity, simplicity, and humility. (He once told me how, on one of his many plane trips, the stewardess was having a lot of trouble with a rowdy in the seat behind him. Finally she whispered to this character spouting obscenities, "Do you know that's Billy Graham sitting in front of you?" Thereupon the drunk leaned right over and said, "Billy Graham, I've always wanted to thank you for what you've done for me!")

About this same time I found myself caught in the middle of the battle that was joining between the "evangelicals" and the "activists." It seemed that "evangelical" referred to the churches and preachers who believed that the sole task of the Church was to seek the salvation of individuals and build them up in the faith through prayer and Bible study, while "activist" applied to those attempting to relate the Gospel to social and political questions by taking active part in demonstrations on behalf of justice for the oppressed, or by issuing pronouncements on contemporary issues. From the viewpoint of our Calvinist tradition, I have never seen how either of these two positions could masquerade as our Presbyterian witness. From our reading of Scripture, the Church cannot be conceived of as a group of people solely dedicated to what is called "winning souls," nor can it be envisioned as chiefly a political lobby. The biblical Gospel is not confined to the liberation of the soul, nor is biblical "salvation" confined to the sphere of individual conversion to Christ. At the same time, we are warned against making the Gospel a tool for establishing the Kingdom of God on earth. Fortunately, I found many leaders who deplored this particular confrontation of two distortions of historic Christianity. And over the years I believe the party spirit is diminishing and the Presbyterian Church is becoming more comprehensive in its leadership as it recovers the truly biblical perspective of the Reformed faith.

There was another temptation, however, that could have diverted me from this challenge. The temptation was to be simply the imported Scottish preacher with all the exaggerated reputation that it implied in the United States at the time. This was a period which could be unkindly described as the sunset of the so-called Prince of the Pulpit. Even in New York the many strong congregations that still existed had their Sunday attendance swelled by hundreds of sermon-tasters who drifted from church to church sampling the preachers. Our one morning service at eleven o'clock was usually full, with overflow crowds in seasons like Advent and Lent. Invitations poured in, asking me to preach in other parts of the country and to deliver invocations at the banquets of a great variety of organizations. (It took me a little time to realize that I couldn't get away with "For what we are about to receive, the Lord make us truly thankful," which is what a Scottish party would expect, but to this day I am shocked by the idea that the Lord needs to be informed about the activities of the society concerned and the importance of the people being honored. Some of the worst prayers I have ever heard have been invocations at presidential inaugurations.) Although I had made a private vow not to use any sermons from my Scottish barrel but to compose a new one each Sunday, it was clear that at that time there was still an appetite for the traditional oratory of the Kirk. (It was about this time that I was introduced at a New York club as "Protestantism's answer to Bishop Fulton Sheen.")

The "angels and ministers of grace" must have been around at this time to warn me off this track. For one thing, I was made aware that the religious boom and the accompanying coronation of the big-city preacher was rapidly coming to an end. The future of the Church was filling up with question marks. In the years ahead, what would happen to a church that depended for its prosperity on the passing popularity of a preacher? Was sufficient attention being paid to the building up in the faith of a community of real disciples? Had the emphasis on stellar preaching diminished the sense of participation in a lively, ordered worship? And how was the Church going to meet the challenge presented by the new secularism, the consumer culture, the growing revolt against traditional values, the agitation for civil rights, the threat of new Koreas, the feminist movement, and the explosion of discontent that was clearly on the way from the nation's youth?

Such thoughts began to impinge on my sermon preparation. When one of our elders very gently suggested to me one day that my sermons might occasionally touch on such themes as Communism, my first thought was, "I'm not going to abandon expository preaching in order to deliver bromides about Communism." Then I realized that this was a false choice. What I needed to do was develop a stronger connection between—to use Barth's metaphor—the Bible and the morning newspaper. At least some grace was given me to listen more carefully to the live, contemporary questions that were in the minds of those listening to sermons. I had no intention of breaking away from scriptural exposition and offering my thoughts on all the controversial topics of the day, but I think I began to understand better how the Bible relates to such questions, and how necessary it is to try to understand what is uppermost in people's minds and let the Gospel speak to concrete situations. The kind of sermon that could be preached anywhere at any time no longer seemed to me to reflect the lively Word of God.

The pastoral background of preaching now loomed larger in my preparation. I was enormously helped by a congregation that shared their very diverse needs and welcomed me into their hearts and homes. Real preaching, I was steadily learning, arises out of an interaction between preacher and people. It is not a matter of implying, "Here's the word of God as I find it in the Bible; take it or leave it."

One other conviction was growing in me during those first years in New York: the absolute centrality of a strong service of worship—welcoming yet dignified, traditional yet contemporary, with the maximum of participation by the congregation, and all directed to the glory of God. That meant an emphasis on the sacraments of baptism and the Lord's Supper, and an effort to recover the rhythm of worship as moving from the celebration of God's glory, through confession of sin, to the hearing of the Word (Scripture, preferably from the Old Testament, the Epistles, and the Gospels), followed by the sermon, then the response in offering and thanksgiving, intercessions, and dedication. I was fortunate to find a rich tradition of worship in our church; a reading of innumerable bulletins from across the country revealed the most extraordinary confusion, with a hodgepodge of glorias, creeds, hymns, anthems, and doxologies all leading up to the great climax of the sermon. Almost always there was only one lesson, usually divided from the sermon by a gulf of other items. I have also been conscious of the tremendous importance of music in the Christian liturgy and feel the importance of establishing a good relationship with the organist and choir director. I was thankful to have this experience as I settled into my new charge.

As I moved into my second decade, I became more aware of the precarious position of any Protestant church in New York City. As the tides of popular religion receded across the country, as church-attendance statistics began to drop dramatically between 1965 and 1975, as sermon-tasters became a vanishing species, as the ominous words "God is dead" began to appear in the headlines, and as schools and colleges exchanged their packed compulsory services of worship for little groups of seekers gathered around a guitar, the writing was already on the wall. I didn't lose any sleep over the notorious new fact that practically any church in the city, no matter how prestigious its reputation, could go out of business in five years if something went wrong. I believe there is grace given to reject that kind of worrying. (I have plenty of sins and worries to confess, but you don't want to hear about them.) Yet this was a decade that did see the virtual disappearance of a considerable number of churches and the shrinking of others to a shadow of their past glories. I noticed that the attempt to recover by spending endowments on social and cultural experiments seldom led to any increase in the worshiping congregation. I therefore became even more sure that the upbuilding of a strong worshiping congregation, nourished on the Word, remains the first priority.

However, the second decade was not only a time of holding the fort and praying for a swing in the religious pendulum. It was an exciting time as the demands for change and a more active participation in questions of justice and civil rights and the criticisms of the "bourgeois morality" began to hit the churches. It was also an agonizing time as the Vietnam War began to hover like an ugly cloud over the entire nation. Once more I found myself caught in the middle: I was quite unable to accept the "Now" generation, with its repudiation of all tradition in morals or religion and its uncritical acceptance of what was called "the relevant," but I was equally unsympathetic with the hysterical reaction of the champions of the status quo. I was aware of the need for some changes in our forms of worship and the antiquities of some of the language we used in church, but I was not prepared to dismantle the liturgy of a church which claims to be *both* catholic and reformed. I was conscious of the need for the Church to stop muffling the Gospel in language and ceremonies that sounded antique and incomprehensible. Yet I was even more conscious of the need to preserve the sense of the holy and of the overarching presence of God in our increasingly secularized society. I resisted the trend toward making the life of the Church a social club or a service institution with a vaguely religious flavor, and the communication of the Gospel a matter of explaining away the mysteries of the faith. A church, I felt, should spread its wings to encompass all kinds of activities in meeting the needs of the neighborhood, tackling such questions as housing, the drug scene, prison reform, criminal justice, and street crime, and offering opportunities for art, music, drama—not merely as propagandistic efforts on behalf of church membership but as genuine ways of relating the Gospel to the culture of our time. But all this activity must spring from the bright center of a living worship and a growing understanding of the Lordship of Christ.

By the mid-seventies the desire for a religion that was not quite so busy and was much more concerned with spirituality was apparent. Unfortunately, many Protestants had gotten out of the habit of looking to the churches for any kind of mystical experience, and so there was a drift toward cults, ancient and modern, that offered either dramatic experiences of what came to be known as "the charismatic," or techniques of meditation and self-discovery under the guidance of some guru. The last ten years have also been years of a new sense of doom. For some reason, the appalling threat presented by the existence of weapons of mass destruction (which has been hanging over our heads since 1945) has begun to become acute. Critics of the new search for spirituality have therefore portrayed it as an avenue of escape, a hiding place from the disaster coming upon the brave new world of technology. While in the sixties I had felt the necessity to stress the eternal dimension and the devotional life, by the late seventies I felt it necessary to speak of the Christian activism that is a necessary response to the Gospel. I find the eighties especially exhilarating because there are signs that the mainline churches are moving off the sidelines and attracting a new generation of those who want to come home to a church that stands for the historic faith, offers lively worship and nurture in the Christian way, is alive to the questions of the day, and does not insult the intelligence.

During these years I have been increasingly troubled by the false choices that are being offered to our fellow citizens. What I mean by false choices is the impression given in our society that either one must be an amiable agnostic, tolerating all kinds of beliefs but committed to none, or else one must surrender to the claims of churches or sects that claim to have the whole truth not only about life in this world but about life in the next, and insist on a pattern of behavior that most normal people cannot accept without hypocrisy. I am speaking about the choice between agnosticism and fanaticism, and I confess that, if I were one of the churchless seekers listening to some of the religion that fills the airwaves, it would make me an atheist. So I am more and more concerned that the historical churches should recover from what I call a loss of theological nerve; boldly stand for the catholic faith as expressed in the creeds; be willing to confront the materialist and secularist philosophies reflected in academia, in arts, and the media; and demonstrate that the Christian Gospel is not an escape hatch for the timid, a drug for the depressed, nor a suicide pact for the intellect, but is still the most morally challenging, the most spiritually refreshing, and the most mentally satisfying Good News that ever sounded on this planet.

From the beginning my call to preach carried the implication that I would be an evangelist. But what is an evangelist? One who thrusts his or her religious opinions on others without a trace of grace? Or one whose main object is to win converts for a particular church? If these are evangelists, it is clear that Jesus wasn't one. Yet he took it for granted that his disciples would want to convey to others the truth that had come to mean so much to them. He repudiated the religious fanatics who, as he said, "would compass sea and land to make one proselyte, and when he is made, you make him twofold more the child of hell than yourselves," but he said to his disciples, "Go . . . and make disciples." And they did. Those who scorn evangelizing might remember that, if the disciples hadn't done so, Christianity might never have come our way. Thus, as a young man, I took part in missions of various kinds, designed to present the Gospel to my contemporaries. Some of these activities may now seem to me to have been crude and occasionally to have resembled the proselytizing that Jesus condemned. I was never happy with the attitude that everyone outside of our own Christian circle was doomed, or, as so many like to say these days, "unsaved"—a word, incidentally, not to be found in the Bible.

In prison camps my evangelism had to be determined largely by the hard task of simply being a Christian in awkward circumstances. But I found a wonderful opportunity to speak to the agnostic, and more often, the nominal church member, about the meaning of the Gospel in terms they could understand—that is, the situation in which we all shared. That was the object of the series of lectures I gave, later published as *Prisoners' Quest.* In my ministry in Scotland I worked with teams who sought to revive the faith of lapsed church members and to use every method to get the challenge of the Gospel across to the unbeliever. I began to think through the question of pre-evangelism, by which I mean trying to change the cultural and intellectual climate so that the Gospel can be heard again by those whom Schleiermacher a hundred years ago called "the cultured despisers of religion." We need Christian dramatists, Christian poets and novelists, Christian comedians. By that I don't mean the prostitution of the arts in the service of the Church, or the production of disguised propaganda for the faith. I mean a genuine appearance on the cultural scene of men and women writing from a Christian point of view. In his *Preface to Morals,* published in 1929, Walter Lippmann acknowledges the immense influence of what he calls "the Christian tale" (the life, death, and resurrection of Jesus) on the artistic and cultural flowering of Western civilization for a thousand years, but regrets that it can no longer be accepted and that nothing has taken its place. I think he might be surprised at the vitality of religion, good and bad, over fifty years later. Gradually it is no longer being taken for granted that orthodox Christian beliefs are incompatible with the mind of the philosopher, the outlook of the scientist, or the spirit of the artist.

My experience in America has given me second thoughts about some methods of evangelism, and my increasing contact with adherents of other faiths has modified some of my theological opinions, but I am more than ever convinced that there is one area of pre-evangelism that has been sadly neglected by the churches. I'm talking about radio and television. Shortly after arriving in this country, I was invited to give talks on the radio and do some television shows, mostly interviews. I gladly accepted such invitations, including the one to succeed Dr. Ralph Sockman on the National Radio Pulpit. As I have indicated, broadcasting is a way to reach the ears and the eyes of people who would never think of entering a church. Broadcast services should never be thought of as "a church of the air," but through them thousands may actually be led to some kind of Christian decision and then relate to a neighboring church, and millions, I believe, can be led to take seriously the Christian alternative in an age of competing philosophies and, sometimes, sheer apathy.

We have yet to realize the enormous effect of television on this generation, and I believe the churches have failed to seize this opportunity for the communication of the Gospel. What I found in America was that the use of television was enormously expensive, except for occasional time offered by local stations. In Britain the BBC allotted fairly generous amounts of time for religious programming and collaborated seriously with the churches. In addition, when the BBC had a monopoly, there was little chance of fringe cults being heard or seen on the air. And, at that time, there were no commercials. When I came to the United States, I accepted the new "book of rules," and I am not about to argue for or against the commercial system here. What I have come to believe is that the vast amounts of money that the churches have spent on other tasks—first on buildings during the period of "the edifice complex" and later on such operations as "restructuring" and multiplying bureaucracies—should have been devoted to buying prime time, to finding and training first-class television personalities from our churches, and to discovering writers and producers who could attract the viewers. I still hope that this can be done.

My experience over the years in New York has led me in the direction of bridge-building in the service of the Gospel. Some of these bridges have led into territory hitherto unknown, but one of them I have just described—building a bridge between the historic churches and the world both of the intellectual and of popular culture, and a bridge reaching across to the media that shape so much of our thinking. I am a founding member of the Society for the Arts, Religion and Contemporary Culture, which for over twenty years (on a shoestring budget) has brought together theologians, writers, dramatists, artists, and creative people of all kinds. I have tried to make theater and movie people, journalists, and artists feel at home in our church. I believe also in building bridges to the political world, not in the interest of supporting particular candidates but in order to express the concern of the Church in local and national politics and to sympathize with those who are performing a necessary job but who are usually rewarded with obloquy and taxi-driver abuse. I want to build bridges in the direction of people in trouble who may feel the church is not for them, and toward those around us who stream past our church every day with never a thought that anything going on there could possibly be of interest. I want to build bridges to the new youth culture—whatever it is—and to those who cling to the image of "the Ugly Presbyterian," the Malvolio to whom Toby Belch says, "Dost thou think, because thou art virtuous, there shall be no more cakes and ale?"

Being a preacher and pastor in the eighties offers exciting possibilities for such bridge-building, and there is one I haven't yet mentioned that has been revolutionary in my experience of "this grace given": my relationship to people of other religious communions—in particular, Roman Catholics and Jews. When I left Scotland, the barrier of ice that separated Catholics and Protestants was just beginning to thaw. The Reformation in Scotland had been a violent one that had left deep scars. The situation was complicated by the fact that the great majority of Scottish Catholics were from Ireland. As a boy in Scotland, I had the impression that Catholics were somewhat sinister people probably up to no good—except, of course, for the few I really knew. As a student I had few contacts with Catholics except when some distinguished figure like Father Ronald Knox or G. K. Chesterton might arrive. We perceived them as searching for converts and thought it unlikely that they would find Edinburgh as fruitful a ground as Oxford. Even in seminary, although we duly read texts of Augustine and Aquinas and studied the edicts of the Councils, there was no live intercourse with Catholic seminarians or their professors. One passing remark of a revered professor sticks in my mind: "Gentlemen, I admire the piety of the Roman Catholic Church— and I detest its politics." That, for me, was that.

I hasten to say that Protestant-Catholic relationships in Scotland since World War II (during which chaplains were thrown together in situations where the labels meant less and less) and especially since Vatican II have undergone a sea change. Recently, for example, the Moderator of the General Assembly greeted the Pope at the Assembly Hall. Ecumenical services are common, students meet freely to discuss theological topics with no holds barred, and the Chair of Divinity at New College is now occupied by a Roman Catholic scholar. On my arrival in New York, I was immediately aware of the great predominance of Catholics—quite the opposite from Scotland—and somewhat shocked that Protestant and Catholic clergy had so little to do with one another. I even found church members who thought of Catholics as belonging to another religion altogether. All this has changed, of course. In recent years I have been reading books by Catholic scholars at least as often as books by Protestants, have shared with priests in marriages and baptisms, and have preached in many well-known Catholic churches. In fact, we are now beyond the point of thinking such things strange. At clergy gatherings recently

I have enjoyed lively discussions without even knowing in each case whether a Catholic or a Protestant was speaking. A few years ago, on Reformation Sunday, I delivered a sermon entitled "A Protestant Writes to the Pope." It was a plea that he might issue an encyclical calling on all Christians, whatever their tradition, to renew their vows of loyal discipleship to Christ. This was not an earth-shattering event, but I was glad that no one in our church raised any objections to this overture to Rome—indeed, many suggested that the letter actually be mailed. A word with a Jesuit friend, and the letter duly found its way to the Vatican. Unfortunately, His Holiness, though sympathetic, found, like many others in such a position, that "the time was not ripe."

An even more revolutionary experience for an imported Scot was for the first time to really get to know rabbis and to recognize Judaism as a vital, contemporary faith. But this will require another chapter, in which I will try to describe some of the travels of mind as well as the world travels that have always been the passion of this wandering Scot.

Chapter Eight

MY
RESTLESS
HEART

It has occurred to me while setting down these scattered recollections and reflections that one might draw the conclusion
that living by grace seems to involve an inordinate amount of
travel. Well, it has for me, and I comfort myself that the same
could be said for Saint Paul. Almost every Bible I own has a
little map tucked away at the back called "The Journeys of Saint
Paul." Yet, of course, there was James, the Lord's brother, who
seems to have stayed in Jerusalem and guided the Church there
until his martyrdom about 70 A.D.; Paul visited him shortly
after his conversion. There is no reason to suppose that grace
is always an uprooting force that makes for restlessness in the
life of a Christian. There were the Pauls and the Augustines,
the John Donnes and the John Wesleys, who roamed far and
wide. But there were also James and those who stayed on with
him in Jerusalem, and a multitude of devoted parish priests
and ministers ever since, like Goldsmith's country parson:

> A man he was to all the country dear,
> And passing rich with forty pounds a year;
> Remote from towns he ran his godly race,
> Nor e'er had changed, nor wished to change his place.

There is room for the roamer and room for the stay-at-
home in the covenant of grace. I remember an occasion in

Edinburgh when two of my professors appeared as the principal speakers. One was known for his indefatigable travels on ecumenical and ecclesiastical business of all kinds. The other seldom left Edinburgh, where he attended to his classes decade after decade and wrote books which carried his thoughts to distant places. When the first rose to speak, he had a lot to say about the benefits of travel, especially for seminarians, and concluded with a quotation from Shakespeare: "Home-keeping youth have ever homely wits." His colleague, steeped in Old Testament wisdom, then arose and cited a verse from the Book of Proverbs: "The eyes of a fool are in the ends of the earth." I shall have more to say shortly about the wanderlust that has been in me since childhood. (My mother used to recount how at the age of two I insisted on walking up the gangway of the ship that transported us every summer from Scotland to Ireland. For me it was the supreme delight of the year—the train to Glasgow, the cab to the Broomilaw docks, the little cabin that held the four of us, and the awakening in Belfast Lough.) Meantime, let me turn to another aspect of travel with which grace has everything to do. I mean the explorations of the mind, the adventures of the spirit, the concept of life itself as a pilgrimage, a constant search for the way, the truth, and the life—with always more to come. That kind of restlessness is, I believe, a real "means of grace."

That brings me back to my inward travels into new territories and the changes that I now see were occurring during my years of ministry in New York. None of these changes was catastrophic. There was no point at which I felt that the foundations were shaking. None of the convulsions—social, political, or theological—of the sixties and seventies led me to question the reality of the grace of God or of my call to preach "the unsearchable riches of Christ." I don't mean that I dismissed with disdain every wind of change that was blowing, or felt like the hymnwriter when he wrote the line "change and decay in all around I see," but I could still sing with fervor the next line: "O Thou who changest not, abide with me." The changes that challenged my mind and spirit were those that questioned some of the assumptions that I had lived with for too long. Less and less did I feel able to give an answer to all the religious questions that come to a pastor year after year. More and more I was tempted to give the answer of one of my seminary professors, who often screwed his monocle into his eye and said, "I don't know; I'm not the Holy Ghost." You can well imagine that with the arrival of our son, Rory, in 1969, a great many assumptions about childhood and parenthood went out of the window, and I found myself wrestling for answers to questions I hadn't even known existed.

Although I reacted rather crossly to a book like Bishop Robinson's *Honest to God* (which was a best-seller in the sixties) and to some of the implications of Harvey Cox's *Secular City*, I tried to listen to the voices that were questioning the kind of neo-orthodoxy into which I had been settling down. It was good to have summer vacations to tackle books that stretch the mind. The continuing influence of Dietrich Bonhoeffer fascinated me, even if I felt that he was often being grossly misunderstood. Phrases like "religionless Christianity" and "mankind come of age" seeped into the pulpits, often with what seemed to me were perverse interpretations. Bonhoeffer's call for an adventure of the spirit was for me a rethinking of the meaning of discipleship, a repudiation of a false apologetic, and not at all the "new modernism" that some were hearing in it. I have mentioned one freighter journey across the Atlantic that I devoted to the dogmatics of Paul Tillich, a theologian who had previously had little appeal for me. By the time I had mastered his style and been captivated by the flow of his thought, I had been introduced to a new vision of the relationship between religion and contemporary culture. What was happening was, I think, a gradual expansion of my understanding of some of the implications of the Gospel that I had previously neglected in my pursuit of what I believed to be a radically biblical theology of the Word. Thus, although I disliked the phrase "social Gospel" (as if there could be more than one Gospel), I learned both from books and from my more activist friends that a radically biblical theology did have a lot to say about the social implications of the Christian faith. I was traveling at least some distance into unfamiliar territory when, for instance, I tried to listen to what black theology, feminist theology, and liberation theology were saying. My prayer has been for the grace to distinguish between a response to a beckoning of the Spirit and a leaping onto the latest theological bandwagon, to know the difference between a growing faith and a passing fad. The fad—and there have been many in recent years, theological and liturgical—seems to me a diversion on the pilgrim's map.

But I must return to the point in my journey when I was rethinking my understanding of other faiths and reshaping in particular my image of Judaism and the Roman Catholic Church. As I have noted, there was a sea change in my concept of the latter. I began by perceiving it as a powerful, monolithic body of believers who made totalitarian claims to exclusive possession of correct belief and correct practice, and loomed up as a sinister and unreformed rival in the field of worship, preaching, and evangelism. I ended up by seeing it as a sister Church, one holding to the same basic beliefs and embracing interpretations of the Christian way almost as diverse as those of the Protestant Church. More and more it seemed intolerable that, in a society rapidly becoming secularist in philosophy and exposed to all kinds of strange cults, those who pray to the same God, adore the same Christ, and seek to worship in Spirit and in truth should glare at each other across barricades of suspicion and prejudice built up over the last four hundred years. The same consideration has led me to a deeper appreciation of the Christian witness of the Orthodox Church, especially their reverence for tradition and their emphasis on the dimension of the Holy.

The most challenging factor in my new experience of our Jewish brethren was simply their existence as a living, worshiping, serving community. In Scotland I had never known any Jews intimately simply because there were so few. There was no Jewish boy in my school in Edinburgh. At the University I did establish a casual acquaintance with that remarkable scholar David Daiches, son of the chief rabbi, whose lectures and books have made a mark on both sides of the Atlantic. It is he who remarked that Americans seem to find something irresistibly amusing in the thought of a Scottish Jew. However, I should add that the Scots' lack of contact with Judaism did not mean that we were brought up in ignorance of the Old Testament. On the contrary, unlike both the English and Americans, Scots were made familiar with the Old Testament even as children. I remember as many sermons from it as from the New; it was read at every service, and much of our congregational singing was from the metrical version of the psalms. Everyone knew "The Lord's My Shepherd" and "O God of Bethel" almost by heart. Also, learning Hebrew was a requirement for ordination in the Church of Scotland. We seminarians learned more than we wanted to know about the rites and ceremonies of ancient Israel, although we knew little or nothing about the continued existence of Judaism as a contemporary religion. (I remember that as a seven-year-old I was fascinated by one old teacher who told us that he had once been at a synagogue. What sticks in my mind is his stupendous revelation that Jews kept their hats on during worship.) As I remember, there was practically no anti-Semitism. The accusation that the Jews were the Christ-killers was a slur I never heard during my entire life in Scotland. There was, of course, the usual quota of jokes about Jews, but since we Scots were the uncomplaining victims of very similar ethnic jokes, these hardly fell into the category of anti-Semitism.

In seminary, according to Presbyterian tradition, great stress was laid on a thorough knowledge of every section of the Old Testament and the idea of the covenant people. Yet, once again, there was something missing. In those days we had no kind of relationship with Jewish scholars or students. We learned nothing of the continuing vitality of this covenant people. To put it crudely, we were left with the impression that the Jews were an unfortunate though wonderfully gifted people who had "missed the boat" two thousand years ago. Their only possible hope for a living faith was to become Christians. Even when the state of Israel was created in 1948, I don't remember having any theological reflections on the meaning of this historic act; I saw it simply in political terms as the culmination of the long and troubled story of the British mandate in Palestine.

It is impossible to live in New York without being constantly aware of the social and political presence of the Jewish community. But what began to set my mind traveling in new directions was the significance of Judaism as a contemporary faith. That naturally led to my doing some reading on the history of the Jews since the time of Christ. From the angle of the Christian Church, it is not a pretty story, and I began to understand, for one thing, how Christian baptism must rouse deep feeling among Jewish people. That led to thoughts about conversion. I still believe in genuine conversion (by that I mean a decision made on grounds of conscience and not convenience), and I am happy to receive anyone who has undergone such conversion into our church—while stressing that this is not a repudiation of their religious past but a fulfillment of it. But this does not mean that I regard Judaism as a dead religion destined to be a special target for Christian evangelism. Through contact with rabbis, reading of Jewish theologians, and a fresh look at the section of the Epistle to the Romans (chapters 9 through 11) in which Paul wrestles with the question of the destiny of God's covenant people, I have come to accept the validity of the continued existence of this covenant people as a witness to God's saving purpose for the world. Again, I feel the deep need for Christians to understand the special meaning of Israel. It is not easy for a Gentile Christian, for example, to grasp the profound meaning of "the land" in Jewish thought and religious feeling.

It has puzzled me that in America, where the Jewish presence is more evident than anywhere else outside Israel, there has not been more awareness of the importance of the Old Testament roots of our Christian faith. The Protestant habit of having only one Scripture passage read in worship is one reason for this neglect. Another is the infrequency of sermons based on Old Testament texts or lectures demonstrating the Hebraic origins of many of our doctrines and ceremonies. Thus I welcomed a visit one day from a rabbi who had just been appointed to a neighboring synagogue. He suggested that his congregation and mine meet occasionally to talk frankly about our similarities and differences. He was not proposing the kind of joint worship that pretends that there is no real difference between the two faiths and attains a false ecumenism by omitting the name of Jesus. The result was a series of meetings leading to friendship between people who were neighbors but knew little of one another's deepest beliefs, and some frank discussion of controversial topics including Christian evangelism, Jewish rules about intermarriage, assimilation, anti-Semitism, and the politics of Israel. The rabbi was Arthur Schneier, the founder of the Appeal of Conscience Foundation. I remain vice president of this organization, and the attendant activities have added considerably to my record of travel.

Travel has led me over the years to think in world terms. I have always been attracted to those we call "foreigners," their varied cultures and habits and the languages they speak. Beginning with my first ventures in Europe and through my seminary days in France and Germany, the war years, and my subsequent visits to fifty-five different countries on five continents, I have enjoyed trying to immerse myself in at least something of the culture of each place, while frankly recognizing that I am, after all, a tourist. (Funny how all our compatriots whom we meet abroad are tourists—but we are not!) I may sometimes be traveling on church business, but I have never been what used to be called a missionary and is now, owing to the disappearance of the old paternalism, called a "fraternal worker," although I was strongly tempted to go to Kenya away back in 1938. I still believe in the Lordship of Christ over all the human race and look for the Kingdom in which there will eventually be the culmination of the human story. Yet, as I travel—physically, mentally, and spiritually—I learn more and more that it is Christ himself, and not our Westernized version of the Gospel, that must be proclaimed, and I also learn more and more respect for the few great non-Christian religions that have left their mark on human lives across the centuries. It also stretches the mind wonderfully to realize that Europe and America are not the divinely ordered, permanent bastions of the Christian faith from which a few forays may be made into foreign lands, and that Africa may well be *the* Christian continent in the next century, while South Korea at the moment has the most vigorously growing Christian Church in the world.

I am not an ecumaniac (by which is meant the person who says, "Any religion is better than mine"), but in these critical days—when nations are both drawn closer to one another than ever before and at the same time threatened by destructive passions armed with the most lethal weapons ever seen on earth—what Christian in his or her right mind could go on believing that the only hope lies in the propagation of the beliefs and practices of one particular sect or denomination? I started with a concern for the drawing together of the Reformed churches across the world, which represent about fifty million adherents. So my first ecumenical travels were to conferences of the World Alliance of Reformed Churches. That took me, appropriately, to Geneva, the stamping ground of John Calvin. Then, through the Student Christian Movement, I was drawn into the fold of the World Council of Churches, which was formed at Amsterdam in 1949. All this led me to do to a lot of reading in the theology of other traditions— reading that increased after Pope John XXIII opened the windows and courageously let some fresh air blow in, and my reading and thinking reached out toward still wider horizons. Travel also made me constantly confront the question of how the ethics of the faith should be applied to questions of peace and human rights. That has led me to membership on the Council of Religion and International Affairs (now called the Carnegie Council on Ethics and International Affairs), where such topics are discussed in depth.

Then along came Rabbi Schneier in 1964 with a proposition. He told me that, owing to the tragic experience of his own life (he lost most of his family in the Holocaust), he had determined to do something, however little it might seem, to build bridges between rival nations and to come to the assistance of religious communities of whatever stripe (excluding only the fanatics) in countries where there were religious tensions or denial of rights. His idea was to develop an interfaith team who would travel anywhere for this cause, get to know both religious and political leaders, find out the facts, and see what influence they could have in preventing a recurrence of a tragedy such as the Holocaust. I encouraged him in this project, but I never dreamed that it would grow into a body that has visited Russia, Poland, Hungary, Czechoslovakia, Ireland, Spain, Argentina, and, recently, mainland China, and has access to leaders of religion and state authorities in all these countries as well as our own State Department. I have been with the rabbi and our Jesuit colleagues on many of these travels, and I could fill a book about our adventures and the curious way in which the advent of an interfaith group often results in the coming together of religious leaders who have been isolated from one another. We have also been able on occasion to persuade the state authorities to mitigate some of the restrictions from which religious communities were suffering. We are aware that such official contacts do not provide a complete picture of the religious situation in any of these countries, but we are convinced that it is important to keep channels of communication open—which means that we have invited delegations from these countries to visit the United States. During the time I have been writing this book, my church has welcomed at a service a Chinese student who obtained permission from the People's Republic to come to the United States to study religion under the auspices of the Foundation.

Other travels that have come my way during these years include visits to Japan, the Philippines, and Hawaii at the invitation of the Air Force in order to conduct retreats for chaplains and others. I went with Dr. Oswald Hoffman of "The Lutheran Hour," and we had a great ecumenical experience, not only with the Air Force chaplains but in getting to know the Church in the Far East. Our trip concluded with a front-seat view of the spectacular eruption of the volcano Mauna Loa in Hawaii. I have also been to Tokyo twice to visit the International Christian University in my capacity as president of its Foundation. This school is a remarkable example of the World Church in action. Founded in 1949, it is a unique combination of academic excellence, international character, and Christian outlook. Such opportunities to travel to the Far East open up the mind to the tremendous potential of that area and the probability that, short of a superpower conflagration, the next century may come to be called the Century of the Pacific, with all this may mean for the future of the Christian Church.

In 1968 the West German government invited me to be their guest as part of the cultural exchange program. That year they had selected (for some mysterious reason) the category of radio preachers, and I was their choice. So I traveled with Charles Copenhaver and Bishop Kennedy, and we were given a splendid tour of Germany with the opportunity to see what the churches there were doing in this form of communication. When greeted by burgomasters and church officials, I could usually count on a laugh when I responded by saying that it was the second time that I had visited Germany as a guest of the government.

One evening while we were in Frankfurt, I escaped from the official round of activities and went wandering. Suddenly, a name came back into my mind—Emmert—who had been the Feldwebel in charge at Spangenberg, where I had spent my longest stretch as a prisoner. Emmert had been a good soldier—too good for our purposes—but he had always been fair, even punishing his own men if he caught them stealing our cigarettes. I found six Emmerts in the telephone directory and tried one at random. I reached our Emmert's wife, and she said she would pass on my invitation to come and see me at my hotel. Emmert did so, and we spent a convivial evening during which the conversation ranged far and wide. I asked numerous questions. "How did you find that tunnel?" "Did you know we had a secret radio?" "When you told me on D day that the German radio was out of order, did you guess that I already knew all about the invasion from our set?" "Do you remember how I was delegated by my colleagues to express our personal sympathy to you when your house was bombed out of existence, and you just saluted and said, 'Krieg ist Krieg'?" Finally, I said, "I just want you to know that, though you were too smart for our purposes, we all respected you as a fair and honest soldier." He thanked me and said he knew this must be the case, or I would not have phoned him.

All these opportunities to travel—in war and peace—have enriched my own pilgrimage of grace. As the years move on, I am more and more conscious of being what my landlady in Marburg called me in 1934—a "Weltkind." That's hard to translate, but it means one who feels more or less at home in any part of the world. Thus I have never known the malady we call homesickness. There are two kinds of Scot: the Weltkind, who for centuries has been making himself at home in Europe,

Asia, and America (and, I must add, as an engineer on a ship), and the other, who hates to tear himself away from the briar bush at home. When I travel, I meet the Weltkind—on a Hawaiian island, in Moscow, in the outback of Australia, in Nairobi, in Brooklyn. When I return to Scotland, I meet friends who ask me no questions about the United States but talk of old school times; they always say, "Well, you'll be glad to get back."

It is perhaps not surprising that I have found myself minister of a church that contains members from all over the world and a great many who share my love of travel. It would be easy to draw some trite theological conclusions from all this wandering, to indicate that I have found that human beings all over the world, in spite of intense national passions and vast cultural differences, are sinners in search of salvation. But that, at least, happens to be true. I have already indicated that my internal travels have taken me far from the notion that the world is divided into a group of Christian civilized countries in the West and a great mass of heathen in foreign parts. While I have enormous respect for the great missionary movement in the Western churches in the eighteenth and nineteenth centuries, a movement that led to the greatest expansion of the Church since the days after Pentecost, I am glad that this movement is now seen in world terms and no longer viewed as the exporting of a Western religion to other parts. The world mission goes on, and it is now at least a two-way traffic. We no longer sing "O'er heathen lands afar thick darkness broodeth yet"—not, I hope, because we have ceased to believe in the darkness, but because it is right here around us. And if I no longer believe that a devout Moslem or Buddhist has no knowledge of the true God, that does not mean that I have ceased to believe in the universal claim of Christ, the incarnate Word, the Light "who enlightens every man" (as we read in the prologue to John's Gospel). I am more conscious than ever of the powers of evil at work in every part of the world, and I am grateful for the Calvinist heritage that taught me to expect it. But I am also more aware than ever of the saving grace of God that reaches us in its fullness in Christ alone, and operates everywhere in ways that no church dogma can define and no church authority can forbid.

Grace thus far for me. I am immensely grateful for its presence and guidance, for the privilege of serving as a preacher and a pastor, for the dark parts of my pilgrimage as well as for the joys, for those nearest and dearest who are my chief "ministers of grace" as well as for the multitude of friends my chosen profession has granted me. Grace thus far. . . . That's how I see it; there is no end to the pilgrimage. I don't envisage a future of my own planning, and as I grow older, I am more and more fond of the text that says, "Though our outward humanity is in decay, yet day by day we are inwardly renewed." I have not said much about the inward voyage that is the most important—what Christopher Fry called "the journey into God." I believe that the grace that has come to me thus far has far more to give, and that the pilgrimage we have on this earth is a preparation for a continuing journey in the life to come. For I don't believe in a static heaven—or hell, for that matter. When I think of my prayer life, I realize how short a distance I have traveled. It's been like paddling on the edges of a vast and glorious ocean. So I want to conclude with an extract from a book that has been with me for fifty years: John Baillie's *Diary of Private Prayer.*

> For the power Thou hast given me to lay hold of
>   things unseen:
> For the strong sense I have that this is not my home:
> For my restless heart which nothing finite can satisfy:
>   I give Thee thanks, O God.
> For the invasion of my soul by Thy Holy Spirit:
> For all human love and goodness that speak to me of
>   Thee:
> For the fullness of Thy glory outpoured in Jesus Christ:
>   I give Thee thanks, O God.